The George of Port Seton

Ian Hustwick

Whittles Publishing

Typeset by
Whittles Publishing Services

Published by
Whittles Publishing,
Roseleigh House,
Latheronwheel,
Caithness, KW5 6DW,
Scotland, UK

ISBN 1-870325-78-8

Printed by J.W.Arrowsmith Ltd., Bristol

Acknowledgements

I am greatly indebted to Sue Mowat for providing a copy of the Disbursement Record of James Forrester and the list of Admiralty Court Cases in which he was named which provided a list of the ships he served on. Sue Mowat also gave considerable help in translating documents and was an invaluable source of information on various Admiralty Court Cases.

Professor Peter Payne very kindly took time to read the manuscript and gave advice on sources of information on trade and other matters as well as providing very helpful and constructive criticism. There is very little information available on the actions of privateers in 1710 and I am indebted to Dr Eric Graham, Michael Dunn and Dr. David Alston for providing a wealth of information on this subject and Professor A.D.M. Forte of Aberdeen University for his advice on sources of information on the law relating to the subject of lien. I also wish to thank George Bain for giving pertinent and useful advice and Gordon Turner for translating the Ransom Note.

I am grateful for the considerable assistance provided by the staff of the National Archives of Scotland, the National Library of Scotland, Edinburgh City Libraries, Edinburgh City Archives and the Queen Mother Library, University of Aberdeen.

Tribute must also be paid to Mrs Pamela Bryce who had the task of reading my writing and typing the manuscript and to Mrs Sheena Bowman for the various illustrations.

Ian Hustwick

Foreword

by Professor T.C. Smout,
Historiographer Royal In Scotland
University of St Andrews

The skills, the tenacity and the details of the working lives of our forefathers too often go unhonoured. James Forrester, the hero of this book, was a skipper in a small East Lothian burgh that specialised in the production of coal and salt, and the *George* was his ship, until it suffered wreck off Scarborough in the mid-winter of 1690. Imagine what it would have been like to live on a leaky wooden sailing ship, with a keel about 50 foot long and a breadth of under 10 feet, with five or six crew members for which the skipper was also responsible, away from home for several months sailing to England or the Netherlands in dangerous seas and dangerous weather. Even then there were many less risky and more profitable occupations, but perhaps not many that demanded more skills.

Mr. Hustwick's achievement is to use the remarkable accounts of the *George* to take us exactly into the seventeenth-century mariners' world, to explain how every part of such a ship worked, from the sails to the pumps that had to be kept constantly at work to save the boat from floundering. He explains what James Forrester had to do to clear his ship from customs, how he used his navigational instruments before the chronometer enabled the correct calculation of longitude, how he fed the crew and, in fact, what every item in the ship's accounts means. After the wreck of the *George,* Forrester had other ships, culminating in 1711 in his capture by French privateers off Eyemouth when captaining the *Helen* of Leith. He was held to ransom in Calais. His wife, plainly of no less character and forcefulness than her husband, used the courts to oblige the reluctant owners to pay for his release.

At every step in the story, Mr. Hustwick, if he cannot illustrate his point from documents directly relating to the *George,* uses other contemporary sources to throw light on the subject. So we have a fine book, informed at every step by a scholarship that does justice to the seventeenth-century mariner's work and its economic and social setting. It is in studying the texture of lives like this that the true history of Scotland's people comes alive.

T.C. Smout
17 April, 2000

Contents

List of illustrations

Introduction

In 1747 the Clerk to the Leith Baillie Court required a book to record the Court Diet and asked his assistant to search through old records in the basement where a book was found which had been used in evidence in an Admiralty Court case held over 40 years ago. There were sufficient unused pages in it to suit his purpose and so the book was turned upside down and became part of the records of the court which were eventually deposited in the Archives of the City of Edinburgh.

The original owner of the book was a seventeenth-century shipmaster who had used it to record the disbursements which he had incurred over eight voyages whilst master of a ship between March 1687 and December 1690. This was a book made up of blank unruled sheets of paper which could have been produced in Scotland at this time for use by merchants to record transactions. These books would not have been cheap and in a period where few people were capable of writing and keeping a record the owner would have taken pride in recording his title on the first page. It reads:

> "Jacobus Forrester est hujus libri lecitimus possessor anno domini 1688"
> *(James Forrester is the legitimate possessor of this book in the year of our Lord 1688).*

The record of disbursements which is given in Appendix I commences with entries for two voyages which took place in 1687, which must have been copied from other records when the book was acquired in 1688. The first 25 pages give details of expenditure and income for eight voyages with the 26th page being a summary of the amounts owed to and owed by the owners. The entries for each voyage are typically headed as follows.

> *An account of money disbursed for the use of my voyage from New Port Seton to Rotterdam with a cargo of small coals for the month of October to the first of December 1688.*

A copy of a page from the accounts is given in Appendix II.

All shipmasters had to provide the owners with an account of their stewardship after a voyage which would also give the profit or loss made on the venture. Very few of these statements of account have survived, probably because the greater majority were written on pieces of paper which would have been destroyed once the profits or losses had been allocated between the various parties. Such records as do exist were those of voyages which were the subject of legal action held in the Admiralty Court in Edinburgh. The records of that court, now in the National Archives of Scotland, contain many examples of disbursements incurred by ship masters that are confined to a single voyage. They are therefore of limited value in providing the costs involved in maintaining a ship over an extended period.

James Forrester's book gives the names of the Scottish ports from which the ship sailed: the Lothian ports of Cockenzie, Elphinstoune, Port Seton and Wemyss and Methil in Fife. As the ship sailed from Port Seton on four of its eight voyages a record of the cargoes carried on these voyages would be contained in the custom records for 1688/89 for the Precinct of Prestonpans, which included Port Seton. Custom regulations of that time required shipmasters when bringing a cargo into a Scottish port to swear on oath that "he hath not brocken bulk in the Scottis seas" and to certify that the cargo listed in the entry in the outport record was correct. James Forrester's distinctive signature is easily discernible in the pages of Prestonpans customs registers certifying the cargo of the *George* of Port Seton.

An analysis of the disbursements and the revenue obtained from the cargoes carried by the *George* between 1687 and 1690, and an inventory of a contemporary ship, provided a considerable amount of detail about the ship, its operative costs and the trade carried out during its eight voyages, and this forms the basis of the first three chapters of this book. Because the disbursements only cover a period of less than four years it is not possible to obtain more than a brief record of trade carried out by this Lothian ship and examination of contemporary records of trade show that its cargoes were very similar to those carried by the majority of ships from that area of the Firth of Forth. The owners evidently ensured that it did not stay very long in port for the vessel made nine voyages in less than four years if an earlier, partially-recorded voyage is taken into account. The greater majority of the 80 ships trading outwith Scotland at that time made only one voyage per annum according to customs records. The maintenance costs of the *George* over the period therefore are not typical. They do however show what was involved in operating the small number of Firth of Forth ships with a tonnage burthen of 60 to 150 tons and undertaking two to three voyages a year outwith Scottish waters.

Any narrative dealing with the activities of the *George* of Port Seton would be incomplete without an explanation of the work of its master, James Forrester. He was solely responsible for sailing, navigating and maintaining the ship, loading and discharging cargoes and dealing with customs and port officials. He would have been a person of some standing because of the considerable amounts of money he spent in the ports of Prestonpans, Port Seton and Cockenzie employing tradesmen and purchasing food and materials. In addition, he would have been one of the few men in the area who had a good education and further had proved to be a competent master capable of delivering cargoes to Holland and England.

A search of the customs outport registers for Leith and Prestonpans prior to 1687 revealed no trace of James Forrester's signature nor any reference to the

George. It is however reasonable to state that Forrester was master of the *George* since 1684 on the basis of the statement made on the first page of the Account: "*Paid to John Adairs his dues for each voyage I have made since I had the ship at £2.00 per voyage for eight voyages which comes to £16.*" In 1682 the Privy Council agreed to pay the expenses of John Adair, a mapmaker, so that he could prepare county maps of Scotland and sea maps of the east coast of Scotland. The cost of preparing these maps was met by a tax levied on shipping at the rate of 4s per tun burthen on foreign ships and 1s per tun on Scottish ships. James Forrester's payment of £2 per voyage would have been based on a ship with a tonnage burthen of 40.

The ship made two to three voyages a year from July 1687 to December 1690 and as the voyage which ended May 1689 was made to Norway it is very likely that the same pattern of voyages to Scandinavia and to the Continent was followed in the period from 1684 to July 1687.

The *George*, according the charge levied to meet Adairs' expenses and for the maintenance of a light on the Island of May, had a tonnage burthen of 40 tuns, meaning that the ship could hold 40 barrels or tuns of wine. A record of 1692 given in Figure 22 shows the tunnage burthen of the thirteen ships engaged in trading between the Port of Leith, England and the Continent ranged from 60 to 150. The *George* was therefore unusual in its relatively small size, in undertaking voyages of considerable length and completing so many voyages in a comparatively short period. This reflected great credit on the vessel's master and the quality of its construction. James Forrester would not have been master of the *George* unless he had considerable experience sailing in ships trading between Scotland, England and the Continent. The nature and period of training that he received and which enabled him to become a shipmaster cannot be ascertained. The Masters of Trinity House in Leith would test seamen who wanted to be pilots or masters (Mowat p. 211). The authority of this body would have been accepted throughout the Firth of Forth and any seaman who received their approval would have been employed by ship owners in all Forth ports. It is therefore possible that James Forrester would have been approved as a competent seaman by the masters on completion of his apprenticeship. England did not have a national body as there was in Spain and Portugal which was responsible for the standard which seamen had to obtain before being judged to have an adequate knowledge of navigation and seamanship and in addition sufficient experience under a competent master. It was left to local seamen's guilds to examine seamen at the end of their period of training.

There was no set time that a youth would serve as an apprentice to a shipmaster. The period apparently varied between five and seven years depending upon the age that he started his life aboard ship and his ability to master the craft.

Shipmasters capable of providing training in ship handling, navigation and maintenance, and in addition, how to deal with harbour and customs officials as well as merchants of different nationalities, would not have been all that common in the Firth (Fury p. 150–56). There were not that many masters who undertook regular voyages outwith Scottish waters and therefore able to give suitable experience to apprentices and parents would have had to pay a premium to the master before their son would be indentured as an apprentice. Many youths whose parents could not afford to pay served as ordinary seamen and with ability and hard work became masters. They would have gained experience by sailing in different ships, eventually rising to the position of mate and would have obtained sufficient knowledge to enable them to satisfy the Masters of Trinity House.

It was noticeable that in England in the sixteenth Century a high proportion of masters and mates could read and write. Apparently many were taught to do so by their masters because as seamen it would have been impossible for them to attend school (Fury p. 151). In Scotland however by the latter part of the seventeenth Century there were schools in the Forth coastal burgh capable of providing at least a good basic education. Forrester obviously had a formal education which enabled him to maintain accounts as well as sufficient Latin to write the inscription on the first page of the account book.

Some boys went to sea as early as 12, an age when they would have been physically incapable of carrying out any of the duties of a seaman and it is unlikely that they would have entered into an apprenticeship at that age. It is possible that James Forrester went to sea about the age of 14 after leaving school and would have completed his apprenticeship, if he did have one, by the age of 22. It was accepted practice that apprenticeships finished at the age of 24 although young men who proved capable of acting as master completed their apprenticeship earlier. The next stage in his career would have been an appointment as mate, a position he could have held for some years before obtaining command of the *George*. By that time he would have been an experienced navigator familiar with the entrances to all main North Sea ports and capable of dealing with both harbour authorities and agents of merchants in several European countries.

As the customs records for Leith and Prestonpans do not exist after 1691, it is impossible to find out if Forrester was master of another ship immediately after the loss of the *George* in 1690. There are, however, statements in two court cases which recorded that he was a master of a ship, also called the *George*, in 1698 and 1699. It is therefore reasonable to assume that he was employed as a master for some time between 1691 and 1698. In 1703 James Forrester is recorded as master and owner of the *George of Prestonpans* and in 1707 as skipper of the *George of Port Seton*. It is likely that they were the same vessel with different owners.

Thus, James Forrester's career as a shipmaster after the wreck of the *George* in 1690 is recorded in various Admiralty Court records as follows (National Archives of Scotland references, Admiralty Court (AC)).

1698/99	Master	*George of Port Seton*	9/377 and 10/109
1703	Master	*George of Prestonpans*	9/13/1
1707	Skipper	*George of Port Seton*	8/87

| 1710 | Master | *Henrietta of Leith* | 9/356 |
| 1711 | Master | *Helen of Leith* | 9/400,402 |

The dates of the court cases do not necessarily correspond to the dates when he was master as they may have been held some time after the events leading to the case. He does, however, seem to have served in at least four different ships as master, owner and shareholder over the 12-year period which ended in 1710. As stated arlier, James Forrester's record of service at sea would have started when he was about 14, and would have covered a period of at least 10 years as apprentice seaman and mate while he gained experience before becoming master of the *George* in 1684. The fact that he served on different ships over a comparatively short period was not unusual, for it was the practice at that time for masters to move from one ship to another. These changes may have been due to several reasons, for example, the ship being sold or wrecked, a young master moving to a larger ship for experience and more money, or an older master wanting a less arduous existence and taking command of a ship engaged in coastal trading. In such a small area as the Lothian ports a competent and experienced master would be unlikely to be out of work for very long. By 1711 Forrester would have been in his 50s, perhaps unfit for long voyages, and may have taken command of a smaller ship.

The statement in the last page of the record of disbursement makes it clear that James Forrester did not have shares in the *George*, although it was common practice for shipmasters to purchase shares in their ships. It was a system with much to commend it as the master had a direct interest in ensuring that the ship was well maintained, cargoes were delivered in good condition and expenditure was kept at a low level. Forrester is recorded as a shareholder of at least three ships in several court cases, although there is no record that he was a shareholder in the *Helen*, which was captured by the French in 1710. The last entry in Court records relating to James Forrester was his capture by a French privateer in 1710. The ship was freed to continue her voyage after Forrester agreed to pay the ransom, and he was taken as hostage to a prison in Calais. Janet Johnston, his wife, knowing that he would remain there until the end of the war unless the ransom was paid, approached the owners without success. In an act which must have taken considerable courage, she raised an action in the Admiralty Court to force the owners to pay the ransom. The events leading up to the trial and its outcome are set out in Chapter Five. James Forrester's name does not appear in Court Records after 1711 and as Customs records are not available for some time after that year it is not possible to ascertain if he was Master of any vessel on his return to Scotland.

Chapter One

The ship and all her parts

Tonnage of the *George*

The customs registers of this period did not show the tonnage of ships and as the *George* was not involved in any court cases where that measure may have been provided it was necessary to examine the accounts for means of determining tonnage of the ship. Four payments were made for charges which were based upon the tonnage burthen of the ship and these were for dues for the upkeep of the Light of May and payment to John Adair, mapmaker. The rate per ton for a Scottish ship was 1s in both cases and this gave the tuns burthen as 40. The term 'tuns burthen' was a measure of the capacity of a ship's hold and was equivalent to the number of barrels, or tuns, of wine that a ship could carry. The tuns were the same size throughout Northern Europe and took up 56 cubic feet in a hold. A considerable amount of wine was transported from the Continent to Scotland and England and this measure of capacity became the basis on which customs, port and other charges were based.

However, this measure of the capacity of a ship's hold was not an effective method of determining the weight of a cargo of salt or coal which, in the latter part of the seventeenth century, were carried more frequently than barrels of wine. It was the custom, therefore, to ascertain the deadweight tonnage or maximum weight that a ship could carry by adding one-third to the tuns burthen which, as stated above, was 40 tons. Using this method would mean that the *George* would be able to carry 53 tons of cargo. It was not a reliable method for, as will be seen when the weight of cargoes carried by the *George* are calculated, the actual weight of cargoes on average was approximately 70 tons (Salisbury, pp. 41–51).

Tuns burthen was calculated by taking the product of the length of the ship's keel and its breadth and width and dividing by 100. The measurement of tuns burthen of ships of similar dimensions could still vary because builders used different methods to measure the width and depth of ships. If this early method of calculating tuns burthen is used the keel of the *George* would have been 50 ft long and it would have had a breadth of 9.5 ft and a depth of 8 ft. With the addition of the beakhead and the bowsprit the overall length of the ship would have been over 60 ft.

Not every shipbuilder used the method of calculating the deadweight tonnage of a ship by adding one third to the tuns burthen figure and various formulae for determining an accurate measure were considered during the seventeenth century (Salibury p. 69–75). If a shipbuilder did misrepresent a ship's cargo-carrying capacity it could prove very costly to him. An Admiralty Court case was brought by the owners of the *Hendry of Leith* whose tonnage was substantially less than the figures claimed by the builder.

The action was taken by John Tait, skipper of Leith and master of the *Hendry*, and the other owners, against David Durie, ship's carpenter of Leith. Tait bought his ship from Durie in 1683 for £3 sterling a tun plus 200 merks[1] to Durie and his wife. Its tun burthen was said to be 60 Bordeaux tuns of wine, but when Tait went to Bordeaux he found it would only hold 51 tuns. On his return to Leith, before unloading he got Durie to certify this fact. He made seven voyages in all, and pursued for a refund of the difference between freight obtained from the number of tuns carried and that which would have obtained from carrying 60 tuns. This sum amounted to £27, plus the loss he had made on the voyages by the ship being smaller than bargained for (AC 7/8 82 1687).

It is not known whether the owners of the *Hendry* were successful in their claim. If, however, it was successful, the reputation of David Durie as a shipbuilder would have been severely damaged. The accounts record payments to a David Durie, carpenter, for carrying out work on the ship in 1689 and 1690 and it is very likely that this was the same man involved in the above Court case. David Durie was a well known ship carpenter and in any case where the fact may have been in dispute, it is very likely that the Court would have found in his favour.

It is possible to ascertain whether the old method of determining deadweight tonnage provided an accurate figure by examining the weight of the *George*'s cargoes detailed in the accounts. The cargoes were of salt measured in chalders and coal measured in hoods, hundreds and tuns. These units of measure were represented by different weights in part of England and Scotland and the weights which have been taken produce cargo weight within a fairly narrow band of tonnage. The weight of a chalder has been taken as the London chalder of 26 cwt, the hood as 1.5 tons and the hundred as equivalent to 8 tons (Neff Vol 2 Appendix C). A tun was taken as 21 cwt to allow for dross. Table 1 shows the various cargoes converted to tons and from these figures it is possible to state that the *George* had a deadweight tonnage of approximately 70 tons, a figure considerably in excess of the original estimate of 53 tons.

[1] merk: a coin worth 13*s* 6*d* of a Pound Scots or 1*s* 1*d* in Sterling.

Table 1   *Cargoes carried by the* **George**.

Voyage	Cargo	Weight	Equivalent weight in tons
Cockenzie–Norway	Salt	52 chalders	67
Port Seton–London	Salt	51 chalders	66
Port Seton–London	Salt	51 chalders	66
Port Seton–Rotterdam	Coal	47 hoods	66
Elphinstoune–Rotterdam	Coal	8.75 hundred	70
Wemyss–Campvere	Coal	9.25 hundred	74
Port Seton–London	Coal	56 tuns	59
Methil–London	Coal	not stated	

Construction of the hull

The *George* could have been built in Leith, for there was a well-established ship-building industry there in the latter part of the seventeenth century (Mowat p. 217). The *George* was not a large vessel and it would have been well within the capabilities of the local shipwrights to construct a ship of her size. It was, however, the practice of Scottish merchants to purchase ships from the Dutch, Holland at that time being a major trading nation with a large merchant fleet. It also had a large shipbuilding industry capable of constructing ships to a high standard with the latest in rig development. Many small Dutch ships were unsuitable for northern seas, being built with relatively flat-bottomed hulls required for the shallow water around the Dutch coast. This difficulty was overcome by Scots having ships built in that country to their specification (Smout p. 49). Shipmasters would have opportunity when in major ports such as London or Rotterdam to observe the construction, rig and design of ships. In addition, when sailing in captured foreign ships, a common happening in these times, they would be able to compare the sailing qualities of these ships with their native product. Any shipbuilder would therefore have information available from shipmasters on the latest developments in hulls and rigging.

The timber most commonly used for shipbuilding was oak for the keel frames and hull planking. Pine was used for planking deck and also for the masts and spars because of its flexibility. There was considerable trade between Scotland and the Baltic countries in the seventeenth century with Scotland being a major importer of timber; Norway and Sweden supplied fir, with oak coming mainly from the port of Danzig.

The method of construction employed would have been similar to that adopted throughout the ports of Northern Europe and did not materially change during the course of the century. The keel would have been laid first and then the stern and stem posts fixed to it (Figure 1). The keel would have been constructed from at least two baulks of timber as pieces of sufficient length would not have been available unless it was a small vessel. The baulks were joined by scarfing (Figure 2) an ancient method of constructing long lengths of timber, which gives a very strong joint. As will be seen from Figure 1 the stern post is fixed to the keel and supported by other timber. This area of the hull had additional framing to take the rudder and the planking which finished off the stern.

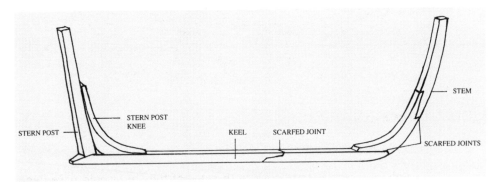

Figure 1   Construction of the keel, stern and stem.

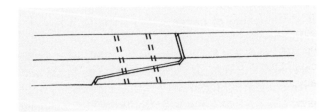

Figure 2   A scarfed joint.

The next stage was the building of ribs piece by piece starting with floor timbers fixed to the keel. The ribs on either side of the keel were gradually built upwards by jointing pieces of timber together again, by scarfing, each piece being called a foothook or futtock. These ribs were constructed in pairs which were bolted together, a system which gave added strength. As the rib was built up to bulwark level the rib became thinner because the rib structure at that height did not have to withstand the same pressure as the ribs at water level (Figure 3).

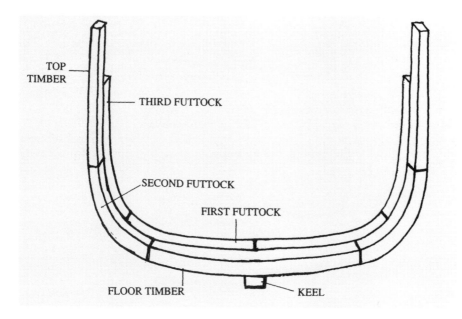

TOP TIMBER

THIRD FUTTOCK

SECOND FUTTOCK

FIRST FUTTOCK

FLOOR TIMBER

KEEL

Figure 3   Construction of the rib.

In larger yards, the complete ribs for both sides of the ship would have been constructed on the ground and then lifted up by means of sheerlegs and bolted to the keel. Smaller yards would not have had large enough sheerlegs to lift these heavy structures and accordingly the ribs would have been constructed futtock by futtock using a pole to lift each piece. The construction of the ribs was a laborious and difficult process as the outside edge of each rib would have to form the expected line of the hull. This would require constant checking with each rib having its surface checked by holding long flexible pieces of timber against the ribs to ensure the rib faces ran true along the length of the ship.

When the ribs had been completed and checked for line, the planking of the hull would begin. These planks, which were as long as possible to avoid butt joints, were first steamed to make them pliable. They were then held to the rigs by clamps and then fixed by means of wooden dowels called treenails, as nails or bolts could not be used because of corrosion. The treenails were hammered into pre-drilled holes, leaving part standing proud of the hull, and a wedge was hammered in the end of each treenail to make a very effective joint. One feature of these early ships was the wales, which were extra thick planks which ran the length of the ship, although the *George*, not being a large ship, would only have had two wales. When the outside planking was completed the inside of the ribs would also be planked, adding considerable lateral strength to the hull (Figure 4).

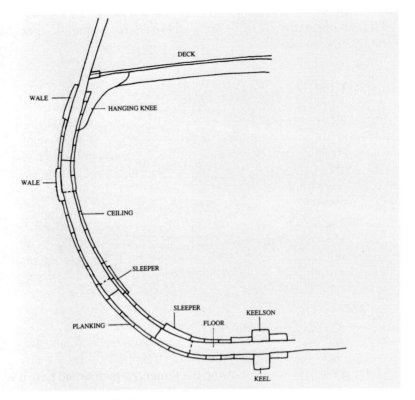

Figure 4   Cross section of hull.

The upper wale, positioned below deck level, had an additional function other than providing further lateral strength to the hull. The standing rigging or shrouds for the masts were attached to the hull by means of chains after being stretched over the projecting wale. This enabled the rigging to be adjusted when it became slack and gave additional support to the mast by increasing the distance between the mast and the foot of the shrouds. In the eighteenth century, hulls were stronger and wales acted more as a protection for the hull when lying against the quay. Rigging, however, required to be placed as far from the base of the mast as possible and so small wooden platforms or chesstrees were fixed to the hull, over which the rigging was stretched and attached to the hull. The picture of the ship in Figure 11 shows standing rigging with ropes called ratlines stretched across them. Prior to the seventeenth century sailors had to climb up the ropes using their legs and feet, so the introduction of the ratlines enabled the crew to climb up and reach sails and rigging more quickly and more safely.

The deck beams resting on hanging knees would then be built, again adding to the strength of the structure. With the addition of deck planking and hatch openings, the hull would be virtually complete. The fixing of the masts into position would be the next task. These would be lifted in stages and dropped into position and fixed on the keelson.

Hull form and fittings

The great majority of paintings of seventeenth-century ships portray large vessels, and if small ships are shown, they are on so small a scale as to be of little value as an aid to determining their hull shape and rig. The probable hull shape of the *George* is based on three ships, two three-masted and the other a single-masted vessel which are shown in *Prospect of Leith* (circa 1680), reproduced by courtesy of Edinburgh City Library and Information Service. (Figure 5)

This drawing depicts vessels with a lower stern superstructure than was common in earlier seventeenth-century ships and illustrates examples of the trend towards hulls with lower stern (Salisbury p. 346–353). A representation of the hull of the *George* is given in Figure 6, showing a ship with a lower stern than the single-masted ship lying against the quay in Leith. The hull is shown with a square stern although some vessels are recorded as having a rounded stern. As was common in ships of this period, the ship would have had a distinctive prow or beakhead which served as a platform for working jib sails and the spritsail (if one was fitted) and if there was sufficient space provision for a 'seat of ease' for the crew. A layout of the deck is also given in Figure 6 showing the fitments which would have been installed in a ship of this period.

Rudder

The rudder was constructed of three or four lengths of timber, probably oak, with the piece called a stock which would be next to the stern port being sufficiently long to extend through the stern of the ship and act as the base for the helm. These lengths of timber were held together by iron bands whose ends were finished in loops called gudgeons that extended beyond the stock. The gudgeons were fitted on to hooks called pintles which were fixed to the stern post and enabled the rudder to swing freely.

Helm

Helm is the Norse word for handle, a good description of this long lever which was attached to the anchor stock. It was a simple piece of equipment and one which could be easily repaired and replaced if broken. An illustration is given in Figure 7. The helm, together with the mizzensail and the square topsail, was used to steer the ship. When these sails were set correctly the helm required very little movement in order to keep the ship on her intended course. In fair weather the helm would have been attached to the sides of the ship by means of ropes, thus freeing the helmsman for other duties. In bad weather the helm would be attached by ropes to both

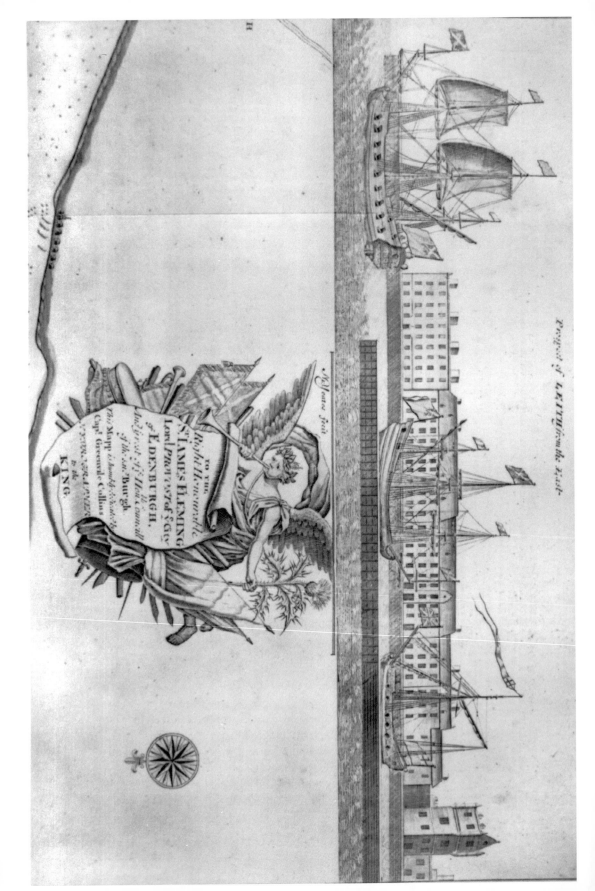

Prospect of LEITH from the East

TO THE
Right Honorable
Sr JAMES FLEMING
Lord Provost of ye City
of EDENBURGH
And y rest of ye Hon.ble Councill
of the sd Burgh.
This Mapp is humbly Dedicated
by Capt Greenvile Collins
Hydrographer in Ordinary
to the
KING.

Ne Yeato Feit

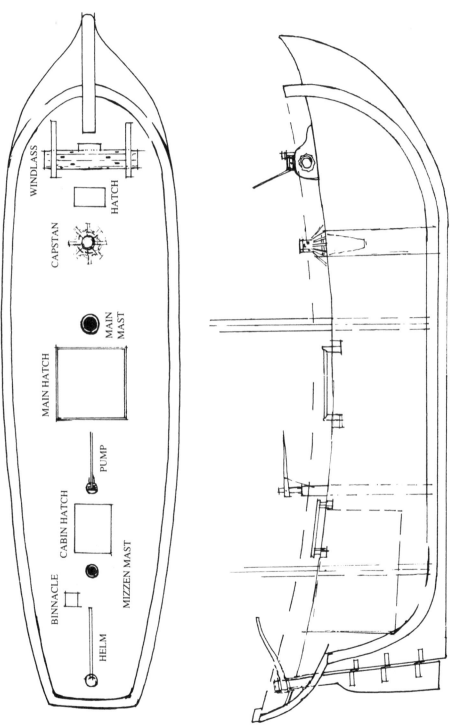

WINDLASS

HATCH

CAPSTAN

MAIN HATCH

MAIN MAST

PUMP

CABIN HATCH

BINNACLE

MIZZEN MAST

HELM

Figure 6   Profile of hull and layout of deck.

Figure 5 (facing)   The prospect of Leith.

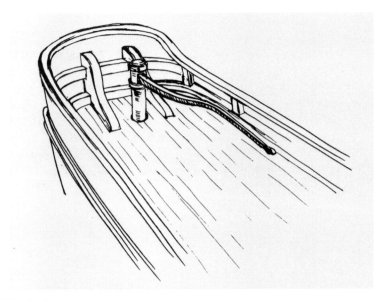

Figure 7   The helm.

sides, thus avoiding extreme movements of the shaft which could cause severe injury to the helmsman.

Binnacle or bittacle

The binnacle, which housed the compass, would be situated to the left of the helm so that the helmsman could check the direction of sailing. This structure is dealt with in more detail in the section on navigational equipment, page 28.

Cabin hatch

The cabin, which provided the living quarters of the master, mate and crew, was situated in the after part of the ship and access to it was by a small hatch on the deck and a ladder. Later ships would have had a skylight, but the *George*'s cabin would have been an unpleasant dark place in bad weather.

Masts

The masts would have been constructed from a single piece of pine, a timber which had the necessary quality of flexibility required for a spar which would be under considerable strain from the sail. Unlike the mizzenmast which was smaller and shorter, the mainmast would have been banded with iron to reduce the risk of splitting and shearing.

Pump

Due to the movement of the timbers of hulls of wooden ships, even well-built and maintained ships leaked, and during stormy weather due to the additional strain on the hull there was a considerable increase in the amount of water entering the hull and gathering in the bilges. An essential piece of equipment therefore would have been a pump to ensure that the cargo was kept dry. As the hull of the *George* would not have been so well-constructed as the hulls of ships built, say, in the nineteenth century, the crew would have spent some time each day at the pump.

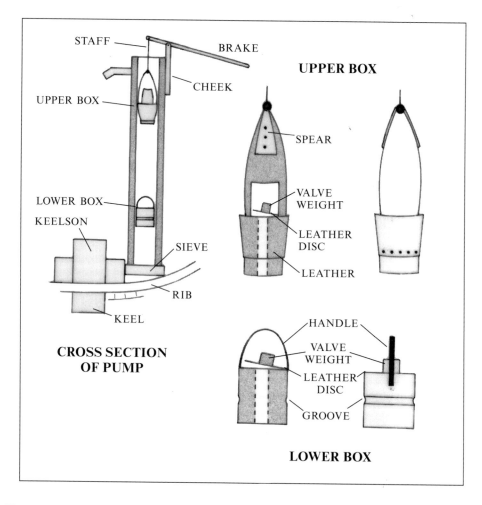

Figure 8   Schematic diagram of common pump and boxes.

Pumps fitted to small ships of this period such as the *George* would not have been very efficient and therefore not capable of dealing with a large intake of water. As an experienced master, Forrester knew it was essential to maintain the hull in good condition and therefore keep the water intake to a low level, and he would have ensured that the inside of the hull would be inspected regularly and any potential source of leaks repaired. The accounts for practically every voyage record payments to carpenters who would have replaced rotten timber and caulked where necessary.

The *George* would have been fitted with a suction pump which was the type commonly fitted in ships of this period and an example of a pump of this type is shown in Figure 8, together with drawings of the boxes which contained the valves. This type of pump had a simple mechanism which was capable of being maintained by the crew and every ship would have carried spare parts so that repairs could be carried out at sea. The inventory of the *George* of Prestonpans included the following equipment to maintain the pump and it is very likely that similar items would have been carried by the *George* of Port Seton although it was a smaller ship.

One pump Kan, one Sliet, five pump bolts, three pump hooks, four pump dials, four pump staves, three lower boxes, one pump scraper.

The function of each of these items is as follows:

Pump kan – this was to hold the water required to prime the pump by covering the upper box and therefore sealing off the lower part of the pump from the air. As the upper box was raised the pressure was lowered within the body of the pump and water then rose through the lower box because of the higher pressure outside the pump (Oertling, p. 22–24).

Sliet – the writing on the inventory is not easy to decipher and it may be that the word is 'sieve'. As the entrance to the pump was situated at the lowest point of the hold any water which gathered would contain solid matter which would clog the valve seating and reduce the effectiveness of the pump. Sieves were therefore fitted round the foot of the pump to ensure that the water entering the pump was relatively clean. The sieve would have had to be cleaned at regular intervals (Oertling, p.30).

Pump bolts – these would have been used to attach the spear to the upper box.

Pump hooks – the lower box had to be inspected regularly to replace the material which was in the groove and formed the watertight seal. To do this the upper box would have been removed and the pump hook would have lifted the box out by its handle which had a shaft long enough to reach to the foot of the pump (Oertling, p. 25).

Pump deals – deals or dales were used to act as a channel for taking water from the pump directly to the scuppers. This channel ensured that no water fell on the deck and passed through it on to the cargo (Oertling, p. 30).

Pump staves – early pump shafts were made by boring out tree trunks, a method which did not produce a smooth internal surface. An alternative method of making a shaft was by using plank staves shaped to make a tight fit. These edges would be caulked and the entire assembly secured at intervals with iron bands (Oertling, p. 14).

Lower boxes – the function of these boxes has already been described. There must have been considerable wear on this box for three spares to be carried.

Pump scraper – the inner wall of the pump would become clogged with material preventing the boxes moving smoothly and so the scraper would have been used when the boxes were removed for maintenance. A scraper would have been an iron disc with holes to allow it to pass through water and fitted with a hook. It would have been lowered onto the pump by means of the pump hook and worked up and down to clear the inner wall.

Materials purchased for the pump

The only item of expenditure which was significant was the cost of work carried out by a pumpmaker which involved the replacement of the upper box at a cost of £4 2s 0d. This was a more complicated item to make than the lower box requiring good quality timber and work by a blacksmith.

Voyage no.	Materials
2	Pump box – presumably this was a lower box
3	ditto
5	1 lb of pump leather
7	Services of a pumpmaker for replacement nails and pump boxes
8	Iron pumps staff
	Pump breck [brake]

The inventory shows that the ship had a water pump which would have been used to transfer water from the quay or small boats to the water casks.

Cargo hatch

This opening to the hold was securely braced to the deck cross timbers and was surrounded by a frame which stood proud from the deck. When at sea this opening was covered by planks, made waterproof by covering them with sacking or canvas coated with tar, purchased each time the ship was carrying salt, in order to keep it dry. This tarred sacking, or tarpaulin as it was called, would have been nailed down round the hatch frame during the voyage and removed prior to unloading the cargo. Cargoes of coal were not affected by seawater and the hatch did not have any additional protection for these voyages.

Capstan and windlass

The *George* had a capstan, as two capstan bars were purchased in Shetland in 1687. It is unlikely that it also had a windlass, because of its small size. The capstan, which was used to raise or lower the heavy anchors, consisted of a barrel which turned on a large round spar which would be securely fastened to the keelson. The barrel had square holes for taking bars for turning it, and on its base there were six projecting ribs called whelps to which were attached pawls that engaged in notches on a piece of timber bolted to the deck. This arrangement ensured that the bars could be locked when the men stopped turning.

While a windlass had a similar purpose to a capstan it was more versatile and was standard equipment on most ships because, in addition to lifting the anchor, it could also be used for lifting masts and spars. Large ships would have been equipped both with a capstan and a windlass to lift all heavy equipment. The windlass had a barrel which was parallel to the deck and was moved by short bars which would be inserted at both ends of the barrel. There were also pawls which were engaged to ensure that the barrel did not move when the crew stopped turning it. Illustrations of a capstan and a windlass are given in Figures 9 and 10.

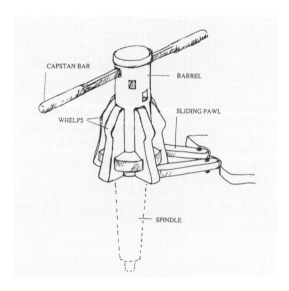

Figure 9   The capstan.

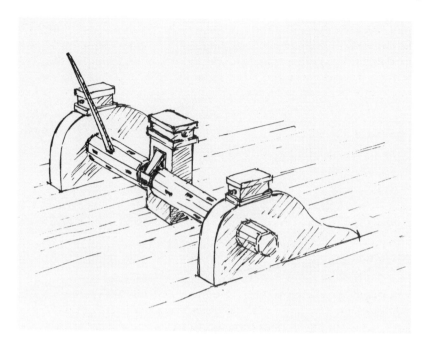

Figure 10   The windlass.

Standing rigging

The main and mizzenmasts would have been secured by fixing the foot of each mast to the keelson and braced against the deck crosspieces. This method would not have been sufficient to withstand the pressure exerted on the masts when a sail was raised and fully extended in a wind. To provide support, masts were supported by permanent rigging attached to the side of the ship, called shrouds. Sails exerted pressure in several directions because of the wind movement, and lateral support was provided by rigging attached to the bowsprit and the stern of the vessel. The bowsprit did not need the flexibility of the other two masts and was a thick post securely attached to the deck beams. This method of securing masts was effective only if the standing rigging was constantly inspected and maintained in good condition. The rigging on the *George* would have been strong but made of hemp, a material which did not withstand wear, and it had to be protected from abrasion by wrapping strands of old rope round it from the running rigging which was used to control the sails. An example of the standing rigging can be seen in the illustration of the ship which is the last one on the right in Figure 5.

Figure 11   17th century ship with galliot rig.

Seventeenth-century rigs and the sail plan of the *George*

There are very few illustrations of ships of the estimated tonnage of the *George* and any reconstruction is complicated because the rigging of ships in the latter part of the seventeenth century was undergoing a period of development. During the next century, rigs for various size of ships were becoming standardised and a vessel with a tonnage of, say, 100 to 130 tons would probably have been rigged as a brig or a sloop.

The only source of information on the sails carried by the ship are the accounts. These list expenditure on two sails, a mainsail and a topsail, both of which were standard sails on more than one type of rig in use at that time. A more useful source is the illustration of ships of the period lying at the quay in Leith, (Figure 5) which is dated 1680.

The two smaller ships appear to have the same size of hull although one has three masts and the other only one. It is unlikely that both had the same tonnage, for a three-masted ship would have had a tonnage in excess of 150 tons because of the larger amount of canvas that she could carry. The single-masted ship is rigged as a galliot (a Dutch cargo-boat in general use in continental waters at that time), with fore-and-aft rig, that is, where the sails of the ship are in the same direction as a line drawn from the bows to the stern. The galliot rig is illustrated in Figure 11. This shows a ship with a mainsail, a square topsail, a foresail or staysail and foretopsail and a lateen sail at the stern.

It is, however, likely that the ship was rigged as a ketch which also had a fore-and-aft rig with the addition of another smaller mast. The ketch rig was similar to that of the galliot in that it had a mainsail, a square topsail which was larger than the galliot's, and a foresail. The major differences were the addition of a small mast at the stern which carried a lateen sail called the mizzen and a small square sail carried underneath the bowsprit called a spritsail (Baker pp. 130–33). An illustration of a ketch rig is given in Figure 12. Although an inventory of the *George* of Port Seton does not exist, there are inventories for two later ships commanded by James Forrester which are included in the papers of two Admiralty Court cases. The rig for the first one, also called the *George*, extant in 1703, is not strictly comparable as this ship had a tonnage burthen of 130 tons (AC 9/42). The inventory does not record the tonnage of the *Henrietta* which, on the basis of the sails carried, would have had a tonnage of 100 to 120 tons. (AC 9/345). The sails carried by these ships as given in the inventories are listed below and correspond, with one exception, the foar (fore) topsail, to those that would have been carried by a ship with a ketch rig.

Figure 12   17th century ship with ketch rig.

The one exception is the mizzen topsail which would have been carried on a ship larger than 100 tons.

George c. 1703	Henrietta c. 1710
One Spritsail	Spritsail
One Foarsail	Foarsail
One Foar Topsail	Foar Topsail
One Main Sail	Main Sail
One Main Topsail	Main Topsail
One Mizan	Mizan
One Mizan Topsail	—

The end of the seventeenth and beginning of the eighteenth centuries saw much development in rigs for various sizes of ships and so the terms galliot and ketch would be used to describe rigs which varied from those given in Figures 11 and 12.

The sails

Mainsail

Smaller vessels of this period carried large mainsails which were difficult to manipulate in bad weather. In the eighteenth century the number of sails began to increase and mainsails were reduced in size making them easier to handle. Improvements in the running rigging, which were the ropes used to alter the position of sails and increase or decrease their size as a result of changes in direction and strength of the wind, meant that the sails were easier to control. The condition of the mainsail of the *George,* as the largest sail on the ship, would have been checked daily, as would all the running rigging controlling it.

Topsail

When this sail came into use in the early seventeenth century it had an additional function to that of providing power, which was to enable the ship to be steered in confined waters. As ships became larger this sail increased in size, becoming in effect another driving sail with its original function being taken over by fore and mizzensails. A main topsail of Carrea duck was bought in Rotterdam for £57 14s 0d. This must have been of good quality as it was considerably more expensive than the vitrie canvas purchased in 1687 for the repair of smaller sails. Sails were made from vertical strips of canvas each 26 inches wide so damaged sections could be replaced without replacing the entire sail.

Mizzen or mizan

The term mizzen is derived from the Arabic word 'Miza' meaning a balance or adjust-ment, which well describes the function of this sail. It, like the spritsail and foresails, was used to balance the effect of the mainsail and for steering the ship. In the seventeenth century the sail was lateen-shaped. In the following century the mizzenmast was lengthened, the shape of the sail became the same as the mainsail of the galliot and a square topsail was added to provide a more effective balance to the mainsail.

Spritsail

This was a square sail set from a yard hung beneath the bowsprit and had a similar function to the mizzen in that it was used for steering the ship. The sail had the effect of drawing down the bow of the ship and because of difficulty in lowering it in bad weather it became obsolete in the eighteenth century.

Inventory of moveable equipment

An inventory of a ship's moveable equipment had to be prepared when a ship was rouped or put up for sale by Order of Court, and the list became part of court records. These inventories provided the only record of the sails, anchors, cables and pieces of minor equipment carried on board ships of a particular period and serve to show that the equipment carried on these early ships was very basic. There is no inventory of the *George* of Port Seton which was wrecked in 1690, and the only source of information on the sails and equipment carried on a ship of this period is the inventory for a similar named ship which was rouped in 1703. This later ship had a tonnage of 130 and thus would likely have carried more sails and would have had more gear. Nevertheless, the great majority of the equipment listed would have been carried on board the first *George* with the exception of the utensils for the cook, a crew member not carried on the ship according to the record of disbursements.

It is worth noting that the master of a late nineteenth-century schooner of the same tonnage would have required the same equipment as his seventeenth-century predecessor; for example, anchors, sails, cables, compasses, hour glasses, lead lines, ballast shovels and materials for repairing the pump. The materials used in their construction would have improved but the use of the compass, lead line and half-hour glass would have remained unchanged, with a log and line being used instead of a piece of wood to measure the speed of the vessel. Nothing, how-ever, would have replaced the skill and experience of the shipmaster.

The actual inventory (AC 9/42), reproduced in Appendix III, is comparatively easy to read and contains at the end a statement signed by James Forrester that the list is true to the best of his knowledge. It was not unknown for these lists to record items which were not on the ship when sold and action had to be taken by the purchaser in order to recover goods or their value from the previous owners. It would not have been an easy task when the ship had several owners not all of whom would have resided in Scotland. Chapter 5 includes an example of an action taken in the Admiralty Court for the recovery of items listed in the inventory.

The transcription of the inventory is given below:

Inventory of the *George of Prestonpans* burden about 130 tons whereof is present Master James Forrester and now lying in the Harbor of New Port Glasgow

Imp: all blocks full with her masts, Hylards and standing Rigging

Anchors

One best bouer [bower] anchor

One small bouer Anchor

One Kedge Anchor

Cables

One best bower Cable of 10½ inches and one hundred fathoms long one third worn.

One small bower Cable of 9 inches about sixty five fathom long with a splice in it half worn.

One hawser about 80 fathoms long half worn

Two buie ropes and four plotts whereof one…

Sails

One spritsail half worn

One foar sail and foar topsail not half worn

One mainsail 2/3rd worn

One main topsail half worn

One mizan 2/3rd worn

One mizan topsail half worn

One watch glass and four halfhour glasses Two Compasses; one Ensign; one Jack one pendant and three wains half worn One sounding lead and one hand lead and line; One pupe [A] lantern and

one iron hand to it One pitch pot; four pitch mops;
three tar buckets; three tar brushes; one gantries,
two wooden buies [boxes]; two ballast spades; four
ballast shovels; one water pump; one water
bucket; one pump Kan; one Sliett [B]; five pump
bolts; three pump hooks; four pump deals; four
iron pump staves; three lower boxes; one pump
scraper; one Axe, one Saw; one Setting Chizel; one
Cabin Chizel; three Katt bands [C]; four locks; one
iron maul; one looming bolt; one plugging iron;
five marlin pins; two worm bolts [augers]; one
Ruge Knife [D]; one great Gun screw; two pieces
of sheet lead; six scrapers; three whip staves; one
bellie for holding pitch and three other bellies; two
hogsheads; one tairce, one tar half full; six new
blocks; two tackle blocks; two cro irons; five iron
hooks; one block with a hook; two pairs of Kan
hooks; one pair of slings; four iron Shott; one new
Capstan bar and eight hand spikes; one Ensign
staff and Jack staff; two small masts and three
small yards; one swab; two gilded trucks;

One long boat; five Oars; one rudder...; iron
rudder pin; two leeboards; one...and iron bolt; two
shafts; two boats...one boat windlass; two pairs
of tashers [E]; a grapline; two Chocks; one mast
and boom and sails.

This I give up as the true inventory of the above
named ship to the best of my knowledge.

**Reproduced by kind permission of the Keeper of the Records of Scotland,
ref. no. AC9/42.**

Note (A)   The pupe or poop lantern would have been situated at the stern of the ship.

   (B)   One Sliet – purpose not known. It may have been another term for sieve.

   (C)   Katt Bands may have been part of the catleads which were posts which projected from the bow and were used to raise and lower the anchors.

   (D)   Ruge or Rugging knife – purpose not known.

   (E)   Tashers – purpose not known.

The inventory of the *George* also gives the equipment belonging to the cook, which has been omitted from the transcription.

Description of the items listed in the inventory

Anchors and cables

One best bower anchor

One small bower anchor

One kedge anchor

One best bower cable 10½ inches and 100 fathoms long

Small bower cable 9 inches and 65 fathoms long

As the name implies, the bower anchors were situated at the bow of the ship with the best anchor being the one in constant use. The small bower was used as an additional mooring aid. Kedge anchors were used to warp or move the ship about a harbour and were normally much heavier than a bower anchor. These anchors would have been lifted by means of the capstan with a cable going through blocks mounted on the catheads, which were beams projecting on either side of the bow. This arrangement ensured that the anchors would be lifted and lowered without damaging the hull. When the vessel was at sea the anchors would be secured to the inside of the bulwarks by katt bands. It would have been necessary to ensure that these heavy items were always well secured, and the bands would have been made to fit inside the bulwarks of the ship. As ships of this period had frequently to be offshore where they were exposed to the movement of tides, currents and bad weather, they had to rely on anchors and cables to ensure that they were not moved. The palms and the shank of anchors of this period were fashioned in iron, the only metal available at this time capable of withstanding the strain of holding a ship in position. The anchors would have been fashioned by smiths who would have specialised in this work. The shank, however, was made of two pieces of timber fastened together by bands of iron. An anchor and an anchor stock was purchased in 1688 at a cost of £28 4s 0d together with a stock costing £4 16s 0d. The high cost of these items reflected the quality of the materials used and the craftsmanship required to make them. Figure 13 illustrates a typical anchor of this period.

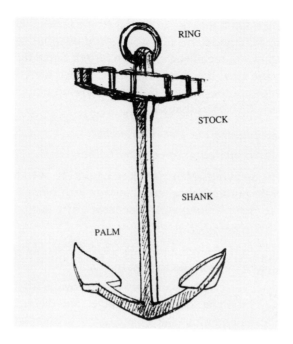

RING

STOCK

SHANK

PALM

Figure 13   A wooden-stocked anchor.

Cables were very thick ropes used to link the ship to the anchor when the ship was lying offshore. Unlike the sheltered waters of a harbour, the seas, even in sheltered waters of a bay, would be high and the cable and its anchor would have been under considerable strain. Hawsers which were the ropes used to attach a ship to a quay, are not listed in the inventory although the *George* did possess them. On the seventh voyage, a new hawser and half a new cable were purchased at a cost of £138 6s 0d. This was the largest single item of expenditure in the accounts and is proof of the importance given to these items by seamen.

The sails listed are the spritsail, foar or foresail, foar topsail, mainsail, maintopsail, mizzen and mizzentopsail. The mizzen had a topsail as did the foresail, all of which added to the effectiveness of the mizzen and the foresail in a larger ship. The condition of the sails is given, half worn or two-thirds worn, and would have been repaired and patched. The ensign was flown on its staff which was mounted at the stern. The jack was flown on its staff which was mounted at the end of the bowsprit.

The hull and the deck planking of a wooden vessel were in a constant state of movement when the ship was at sea, and the consequent small gaps let in water. If the ship was carrying a cargo which had to be kept dry (such as woollens or salt) it was necessary to seal the gaps on the deck planking by running in pitch which was thicker and more flexible than tar. Cargo aside, the crew would have found living conditions very unpleasant if the roof of their quarters leaked. Tar would have been used to seal hull planking when the ship was hauled onshore, laid on her side and the planks scrubbed clean, recaulked and then tarred. Since this work would have been carried out by the crew, the ship would have carried utensils to enable this to be done. The inventory of the *George* lists the following equipment which would have been carried on all ships of that period.

One pitch pot, four pitch mops, three tar buckets

One bellie for holding pitch and three other bellies

The term 'bellie' is an abbreviation of bellied cauldron, used for heating pitch or tar. Barrels of tar were purchased on every voyage with one exception and would have been applied to hull planking when necessary. The last payment for tar was made in London.

Mr White for a barrel of tar and 4 bolts of reids [reeds] £14 12s

The reeds presumably were required to heat the cauldron.

Ballast would have been required on every return voyage when there was little or no cargo, thus making the ship difficult to handle. The distribution of cargo and ballast was very important as most ships were easier to steer when the balance of cargo was towards the stern or midship. A master would know by experience where ballast should be situated and would ensure that the ballast, which usually comprised shingle, would be moved by the crew using ballast shovels and spades, and then confined to specified areas by fixing boards attached to the ribs. Obtaining ballast was expensive because of the need to transport the shingle to the ship and load it into the hold.

The tools carried on the ship were an axe, a saw, a chisel, a maul, a plunging iron and a cabin chisel. The chisel may have been used for caulking although there was a tool specifically for the purpose of hammering oakum between planks. The maul was a large hammer used for knocking out iron bolts. The cabin chisel was possibly a tool with a good handle and in better condition than the other chisel and therefore would have been used for finer work. The crew would not have required any more than these simple tools as any major repair would be carried out by carpenters and blacksmiths when the ship was in port.

In 1689 war was declared on the French and there were numerous French privateers operating in English and Scottish waters. All ships would have carried some sort of armament and, as the accounts show, the *George* was no exception. 'Two firelocks and powder for same' were purchased in 1689. A dozen iron shots for the guns and one quarter hundred powder together with some cartridge paper, small shot and a match were purchased in the following year. The *George* had at least two small cannons and two firelocks and this armament should have been sufficient to repel an attack. Escort was provided by naval vessels on at least two voyages although it is likely this escort would only have been provided on the outward leg when the ship had a cargo. Privateers, however, would capture a ship with or without a cargo and always had the option of ransoming the ship if its cargo was of no value to the master of the privateer.

All ships required a boat, for in these days it would rarely be tied up at a quay and had to have the means of reaching the shore. The accounts record the payment of £22 10s for repair of the boat and subsequently the purchase of oars and a small sail, so it was well maintained. The boat would have been secured on top of the hatch when the ship was at sea and would have been lowered and raised on to the hatch by means of the capstan.

It was customary for ships to show their national flag or that of their home port and the *George* should have flown the Union flag on its mainmast as was required by the proclamation of 1605 and the saltire on the jackstaff at the stern. In Figure 5 the three-masted ship is flying the saltire flag on the mainmast and on the jackstaff so it is obviously a Scottish vessel. The smaller ship is flying the English cross of St. George both on her mainmast and jackstaff, which leaves no doubt of its nationality.

Navigation equipment

The inventory of the second *George* lists the following items which would have been required to navigate the vessel.

> Two Compasses
>
> One Hand Lead Line
>
> One Sounding Lead
>
> One Watch Sand Glass and
>
> Four Half-Hour Sand Glasses

These items would certainly have been carried on board the *George* of Port Seton as they were the basic tools which a master used to navigate a small ship in continental waters and the Baltic in the seventeenth century. At any time during the day the master of seventeenth and early eighteenth century ships would see from the traverse board (Figure 14) the direction sailed by the ship in the last 24 hours. This board was a round piece of wood marked with the 32 points of the compass with holes along the centre to each point, 4 rows each with eight holes at the foot. Using a half-hour sandglass the direction travelled in the period was recorded by inserting a peg on the compass course. After the log was run out, the speed in leagues or knots would be recorded on the traverse board by means of a peg on the bottom row. At the end of the watch, the courses followed during the watch would be noted on the log slate together with the speed or knots recoded.

The half-hour glasses are given in the inventory but there is no record of a traverse board, which may have been the property of the master and not included as part of the equipment of the ship. The earliest recorded use of a traverse board is in the sixteenth century and Captain John Smith in his *Sea Grammar* published in 1627 provides the following description of this aid.

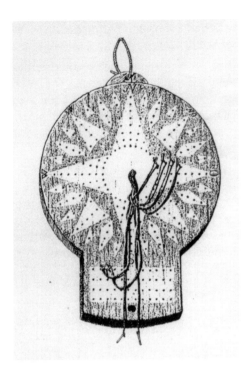

Figure 14   The traverse board.

upon a Bittacle is also a Travas which is a little round boord full of holes
upon lines like the Compasse upon which by the removing [the repeated
moving] of a little sticke the keepe an account how many glasses which are
but half hours they steare upon every point (Smith p. 14)

James Forrester had to rely on the equipment listed above and a traverse board. In addition, he would have had written sailing directions or would have committed to memory the landmarks on the coastline, their distance from his home port, the nature of the seabed, the tides and all other relevant information about the route between various ports. To operate these tools required long experience and good judgement for all the information that he had only enabled him, when away from the coast, to fix an approximate position.

The compass had been used by seamen in European waters since the twelfth century. In its early form it would have been difficult to use at sea as well as being unreliable. Early compasses used a needle which was magnetised by being stroked by a lodestone and then put on a piece of wood. The wood and the needle would be placed in a bowl of water and would indicate the eight cardinal points. In the thirteenth century compasses were protected by being kept in boxes each of which had a vertical needle projecting from its base. The magnet, which was placed on a card which originally showed eight then 16 and finally the 32 points of the compass, was set on top of the needle so that it pivoted easily. The box holding the compass was protected by a piece of glass set in putty so that it was watertight. (Figure 15) Later compasses were set in gimbals so that they remained level when the ship was in motion (Hutchison p. 175–6).

Captain John Smith gives the following description of a compass (Smith p. 13–14).

And in it alwaies stands the Compasse which every one knowes is a round box and in the midst of the bottome a sharp pen called a Center whereon the Fly [card] doth play which is a round peece of Paceboard (paste board) with a smaller wyer [wire] under it touched with a loadstone. In the midst of it is a little brass Cap that doth keepe it levell upon the Center. On the upper part is painted 32 points of the Compasse covered with glasse to keepe it from dust, breaking, or from the wind. This Box doth hang in two or three brass circles [gimbal rings] so fixed, they give such way to the moving of the Ship, that still the Box will stand steady.

The compass on the *George* may not have been mounted on gimbals but just set in a box and covered with a glass. It was still an inefficient and unreliable instrument as it did not retain its magnetism for very long and the presence of large amounts of iron on board the ship (such as a cargo of iron or a cannon positioned near the compass) resulted in significant deviations from North. The *George's* compasses were 'dressed' on four occasions between July 1687 and December 1690.

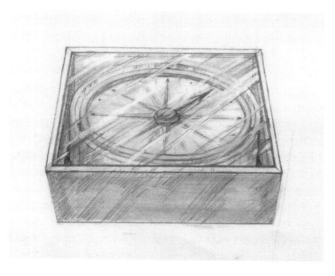

Figure 15   The compass.

This term meant cleaning or repairing and the work would likely have entailed cleaning the inside of the glass, stroking the magnet, checking that the needle was upright and its point sharp, and resealing the box to ensure it was watertight. This was presumably done at Leith, the only port which would have had skilled men capable of carrying out this work.

One of the two compasses would have been housed in an upright cabinet open at the front and situated to the left of the helm so that the helmsman could see the compass dial. This cabinet was referred to as the 'bitackle' in the accounts. In addition to the compass there were two lamps which were required to illuminate the card at night. The practice of protecting the compass from the sea in a cabinet has been carried out for a very long time as the term 'betakle' is found in fifteenth century records, 'bitakell' in the sixteenth century and the modern 'binnacle' in the nineteenth century. The bitackle of the *George* was replaced in 1689 at a cost of £4 and would have been a well-made structure. On two occasions horns for the binnacle were purchased. It is assumed that these were hooks on which the lanterns were suspended.

James Forrester would not have had a timepiece on the *George* unlike eighteenth century ships, where a possession of a chronometer would have been an essential aid to navigation. It was however necessary to measure intervals of time. The instrument which was used for this purpose was the sandglass which had a history dating back to the thirteenth century. These early glasses consisted of two pear-shaped pieces of glass which were joined at their narrow end by a metal tube and held in a wooden frame similar to that used for domestic purposes today. It would not have been easy to keep the glasses secure in a sailing ship and breakages would have occurred frequently. This, no doubt, accounts for the four half-hour glasses which are shown in the inventory.

In the relatively shallow waters of the North Sea a master would always wish to know the depth of water under his ship and the nature of the seabed. This information would be obtained by taking soundings by means of a long line to which was attached a cone-shaped piece of lead weighing 10 to 12 pounds (Taylor and Richey p. 15–16). The lead was hollowed out at the foot and filled with tallow so that it picked up any loose particles lying in the seabed such as sand, mud or shingle (Figure 16). An experienced master would know the composition of seabed along the routes the ship normally travelled and examination of the sand or gravel stuck to the end of the weight would give him a good indication of his position. This method of determining the depth of water was used by the Romans and was certainly used by European ships in the fifteenth century. The weight was always of lead, not of iron or bronze, and was used because it would not corrode; it was cheap and because it was soft and marked easily by rocks provided vital information about the seabed. Its main advantage was its weight, ensuring that it sank quickly. Because the ship was always moving, a weight which reached the bottom rapidly gave a more accurate vertical reading than a line with a light weight (Hutchison p. 175–6). The depth of water and the time the reading was taken would be recorded on a log board. These readings would be taken more regularly when the ship was in shallow water.

Figure 16   The lead.

Both the hand lead and the sounding lead had their lines marked at fathoms or multiples of fathoms by different coloured cloth so that a seaman throwing the line overboard could determine the depth of water without difficulty. The sounding lead, which weighed from 18 to 24 pounds (Taylor and Richey p. 15–16), was used in deep water. The hand lead line, which weighed between seven and twelve pounds was used for depths up to 30 fathoms, was used when the ship was close to shore and when finding channels into harbours. A sounding lead-line was purchased in 1688 at a cost of £3 10s, a substantial sum when compared to the purchase of '24 *ells of vitrie canvas for mending sails, £5 10s.*' As they were in constant use, these lines would have been made of high quality cordage so as to withstand wear and tear.

Thus at any time during the day, a master in the time of the *George* would see from the traverse board the direction sailed by the ship and from the log board would know the depth of water and the nature of the seabed in the last 24 hours (E.G.R. Taylor p. 549–55). This information in itself would not be sufficient to enable him to estimate his position for he would require to know how far the vessel had travelled.

The method used by English navigators since the latter part of the sixteenth century to ascertain distance travelled was the log and line. This consisted of a long line on a revolving drum attached to the log which was a triangular piece of wood weighted on one side in order to keep it upright (Figure 17). The log was dropped over the stern of the ship, a 30-second glass turned and the movement of the line stopped when the sand had run out. The line was then hauled in and the length measured in fathoms by the traditional method of the stretch of a man's arms. If the ship did not possess a 30-second glass then time would have been measured

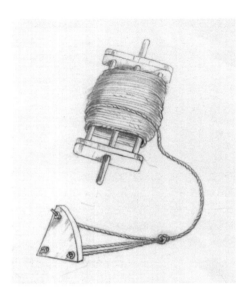

Figure 17   The log and line.

by counting up to 60 or using a set form of words. To calculate the speed the length was multiplied by 60 and divided by 2500 to obtain a speed in leagues per hour and was based upon a mile of 5000 feet. This method was not accurate for various reasons; sandglasses varied in the quantity of sand; co-ordinating the starting and stopping of the line with the turning of the glass was difficult and the length of men's arms could vary. Apart from these problems a more serious error could occur if log did stream away from the ship because it was caught by eddies as a result of the movement of the ship. When this happened no measurement of speed would be recorded.

To overcome the problem of measuring the length of line run out, the line was knotted at intervals of 51 ft based upon a nautical mile of 6080 feet. Some masters, however, used a line with knots at intervals of 48 feet. This over-estimated the speed of a ship making her ahead of her true position, an advantage when approaching land. As 48 feet was equivalent to 8 fathoms it was easy to check the line for shrinkage. The number of knots passing over the counter was recorded to show that the ship was making so many knots or so many miles per hour (May, p. 108–10).

There is no mention of a log and line in the inventory so it is very likely that in common with other small ships of the period the method used to ascertain the distance travelled or the speed of the ship would be that used by mariners since the fifteenth century called a Dutchman's log, as it was commonly used by ships of that nation. A piece of wood was thrown over the side and the time taken for it to pass between marks made in the bow and the stern would be measured by counting or by using a set form of words. The product of the length between the marks and 0.6

divided by the time taken by the piece of wood would have been the speed in miles per hour (Gurney, p. 222–3). This method would only have been a guide to an experienced master and because it was unreliable, English shipmasters used the log and line.

The information recorded on the log slate would only give a limited amount of information to the master. He would be well aware that the helmsman's task in steering a ship in bad weather with a small compass was a difficult one, and that the operation of the log and line did not produce accurate results. Allowance would have to be made for the effect of wind which, unless it was a following one, required the ship to tack or follow a zigzag set of courses in an attempt to follow the set course. The only information that he could rely on would be the records of soundings and the nature of the seabed. The method whereby a master made an estimate of the position of the ship after taking all these factors into account was called dead reckoning.

James Forrester would have committed to memory the landmarks on the coastline, their distance from his home port, the nature of the seabed, the tides and all relevant information about the routes between various ports. As seaman, mate and master he would have sailed the North Sea for many years and during every voyage would have watched the performance of the ship, the direction and strength of the wind and the nature of the sea which varied in different parts of the North Sea. He would have had an innate sense of direction, a trait common to men who had spent a large part of their life outdoors. Using that information he would have a reasonable estimate of the ship's position to check against the position reached by dead reckoning. Like all ships of the period the *George* would not have been a fast ship and Forrester would have had plenty of time when approaching land to check for landmarks and taking soundings at frequent intervals.

A ship sailing from Leith to London in the late nineteenth century and before the introduction of modern methods of navigation would not have left harbour without possessing the *North Sea Pilot*. This book gives detailed descriptions of the route between various points such as landmarks, lighthouses, buoys, the depth of water near ports, currents, tides and distances between various points. Sailing directions such as these have been in use in the Mediterranean since the fourteenth century. The Italians had the advantage over seamen travelling in northern waters in having good charts for the Mediterranean and were skilled in the use of navigational instruments such as the quadrant, astrolabe or cross staff. These instruments enabled them to observe the Pole Star at night and the sun's altitude at noon and they could determine their latitude and obtain the position of their ship. They had further advantages in that they Mediterranean was practically tideless, the weather was better, thus giving them more opportunities to observe the stars and the sun, and there were more man-made objects along the coasts which were an additional aid to finding their position.

The North Sea with its shallow waters, variable tidal conditions, stormy weather and lack of charts made possession of sailing directions essential. Even when masters were capable of determining their positions and had the use of charts (by the latter part of the eighteenth century), these directions were still a constant source of reference. The first guide to mariners for northern waters was published about 1540 from information compiled by Alexander Lindsay, pilot to James V, and was called by the French *Routiers* from the term route. An extract from this *Guide for Leith and the Forth* is given below. The English and the Scots used the more prosaic term Rutter when it first appeared in print in 1528. These directions, although providing limited information, would have been of considerable assistance to foreign shipmasters who, lacking charts, would have found it very difficult to reach a Scottish port. During his long apprenticeship before becoming master, James Forrester would have memorised much of the relevant information about the route between ports such as the nature of the seabed, and in particular the best method of entering and leaving harbours. He would have found out the latest information about tides and any changes to the entrance to harbours, such as sandbanks, before leaving port.

The Privy Council must have been concerned about the position whereby there were no accurate maps of Scottish counties and no sea maps of the coastline. A mapmaker called John Adair apparently had on his own initiative started to prepare maps of the various counties and the Privy Council gave him £100 to enable this work to be completed and in addition to prepare sea maps of the coast. To pay for this work they levied a tax of 4s per ton burthen on foreign ships using Scottish harbours and 1s per ton on Scottish ships. Adair completed a map of the Firth of Forth in 1683 and another of the Firth of Clyde in 1686. The first map was engraved by Moll and published in Amsterdam in 1688 (Robinson p. 162). Adair was a very competent mapmaker and it was unfortunate that he was also a dilatory man and it was not until 1703 that his first and only book comprising six sea maps was published. Each map was accompanied by directions on how to enter every harbour and gave details of rocks and safe anchorages. An example of these directions is given on page 62. These maps would have been of limited use to mariners as they did not show latitude or longitude (Inglis p. 60–66). James Forrester paid £35 10s 0d based on 17 voyages undertaken between 1684 and 1690 and would not have obtained any benefit from these payments as the maps were not published until 1703. John Adair's map of the Edinburgh Firth is shown on the cover of this book.

Sixteenth Century Navigation
Leith and the East Coast of Scotland

Compiled from information supplied by Alexander Lindsay
Pilot to James V, 1540

Leith and the Forth

Tides

At Leith, when it blow, the tides run SSW and NNE.
From Leith to St Abbs Head, when the moon is S by W it is full sea.
From the Road of Leith to the Isle of May the tide runs SSW and NNE.

Courses

1 Heading South
In sailing to the north between Leith and Kinghorn, the South course to the
Bass must be N by E and S by W.
From the Bass to St Abbs Head, the course is ESE and NWN.

2 Heading North
From the Road of Leith to Inchkeith, NNE.
From Inchkeith to the May or the Point of Fife, NE by E.
The May and the Point of Fife lie S and N.

Soundings

If you would stay in the Road of Leith, cast anchor at NW or WNW straight
against the town of Leith, and you shall have 7 fathoms of water at full sea
and 3½ at low water.

Distances

Leith to St Abbs Head – 60 miles   Leith to Inchkeith – 4 miles
Inchkeith to the May – 20 miles   The May to Fifeness – 8 miles
Inchkeith to Fifeness – 28 miles

At approximately the same time that Adair was surveying the Firth of Forth, the Admiralty in London appointed a Captain Greenvile Collins to prepare maps of the English and Scottish coasts. This work commenced in 1681 and, by 1689, 53 maps had been completed and all were published in 1693, together with directions for entering large ports. The preparation of these maps involved a considerable amount of work and it is unfortunate that due to a lack of money insufficient time was given to carrying out the surveys, so that Collins' maps for some areas are not as accurate as those prepared by Adair. The most important feature, however, of Collins' work was that in 1693 there was a set of maps covering the east coast of England and Scotland from Kent to the Moray Firth. Collins' map of the Edinburgh Firth is given in Figure 18.

Figure 18 (opposite) Collins' map of the Edinburgh Firth. Reproduced by permission of the Trustees of the National Library of Scotland.

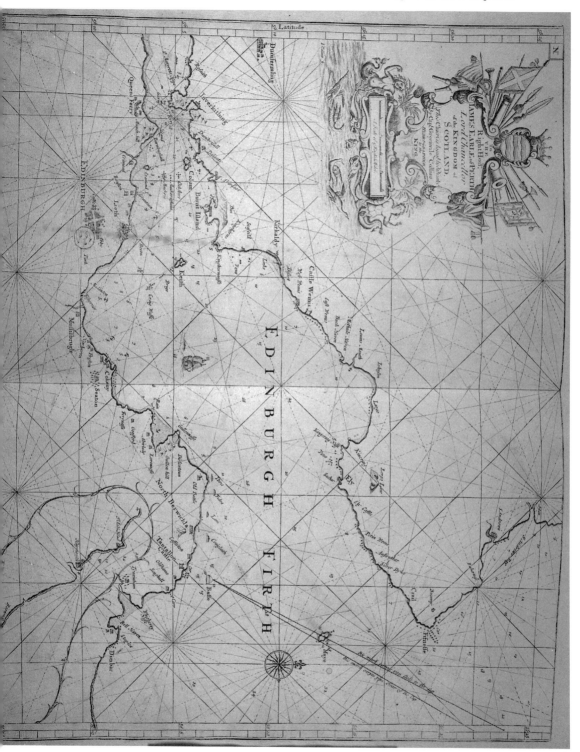

Chapter Two

Disbursements, freight and owners

As will be seen from reading the record of disbursements for the *George*, which is given in Appendix I, the entries in the disbursement record for each voyage were made after each payment was incurred so that payments for beer and bread are followed by an entry recording the sum paid for work done by a carpenter. It is inevitably a bald statement of the goods and services purchased, with occasionally the name of the tradesman such as William Leslie for nails and George Seton for supply of an oak plank. There is, however, no accompanying statement to show the purpose of the work done, and an analysis of the figures only gives a breakdown of costs involved in operating the ship. An examination of the amounts paid for each voyage show variations between the cost of wages or food for each voyage and, as detailed accounts for ships operating during this period are not available, it is not possible to make comparisons and determine whether the crew were paid and received rations comparable with those of similar ships. In such a small area as the Firth it is likely that wages for crews and their rations would not have varied very much.

From the payments made on the authority of the master it is possible to see that he had to be capable of dealing with a diverse group of suppliers of goods and services as well as custom and harbour officials, and that as an agent for his owners he had considerable responsibility. He would have had to ensure that the food was fit for consumption, that the timber used for repairs was well seasoned and that the sails he bought in Rotterdam were of good quality. In 1690 Forrester travelled to Leith on horseback to purchase an oak plank at a cost of £9 10s. He would have ascertained it was of good quality, then arranged transport for the plank was 26 feet long and could have been damaged unless the carter was capable. He then employed David Durie, a Leith carpenter, to use the timber to carry out the necessary repair work at a cost of £21 12s, and a William Forrester to apply tar to the new timber at a cost of £20. He was careful to purchase timber of the best quality and employ skilled men to carry out the repair work. There would, of course, have been some element of self-interest in ensuring that the food and materials were of good quality as he had to eat the same food as the men and to sail in the same ship.

When this diverse record of payments is summarised (Table 2) it is possible to show how much was spent on the crew, the ship, harbour and other charges. The cost of paying and feeding the crew amounted to some 59% of the total. This was normal for vessels of this period due to the large number of crew which was required to sail and maintain the ship and the time taken to complete each voyage. Maintenance of the ship amounted to 26% and port and other charges were 15% of the total cost.

By comparison an analysis of the cost of operating a Scottish-owned schooner of 191 tons built in 1855 gives a completely different picture, with maintenance comprising 30% of the total, wages and food 35% and insurance, harbour charges and brokerage 35%.

This was a much faster ship than the *George* and employed fewer crew, factors which played a significant part in the variations noted.

Food

The food purchased for the master and crew consisted mainly of meat, beer and bread, apparently standard fare for all voyages. Occasionally fresh vegetables, fish and butter were purchased but these items formed only a minor part of the diet, a diet noticeably deficient in vitamin C. As the crew spent most of their time at sea or in harbour with the exception of the winter months, they would have had little opportunity to eat fresh vegetables and probably suffered from scurvy. At the least they must have suffered from indigestion for the ship did not carry a cook and a member of the crew would have been delegated to carry out the task of preparing and cooking the food. No doubt the crew would have frequently considered the truth of the old saying that 'God sent the food and the devil sent the cooks'.

The food taken on board the *George* for a voyage to Rotterdam in April 1689 provides a good example of what was purchased by the master for himself and the crew. Certain provisions were specifically purchased for consumption by the passengers who were carried on three voyages.

	£	s	d
Half an anker of ale		16	8
Half a hundred biscuits	2	18	0
A tierce of beer	3	6	8
Half a boll of beans	2	16	8
4 pecks of groats	3	4	0
6 Swine	39	16	0
1 Ox	14	0	0
Half a barrel of beef	7	0	0
400 lbs of bread	21	12	0
2 tierces & 2 half hogshead of beer	14	0	0

Table 2 Analysis of disbursements 1687–1690.

Voyage	Cargo	Wages	Food	Maintenance	Harbour charges	Sundry costs	Total	Surplus	Loss	Crew	Period	No. of days*
1. Cockenzie Greenock Norway Cockenzie	salt	251	294	132	23	44	744	162	—	7	July 1687 March 1688	260
2. Port Seton London	salt	222	134	195	36	34	621	45	—	7	May 1688 1 July 1688	45
3. Port Seton London	salt	222	118	74	37	36	487	—	52	7	July 1688 end Sept 1688	75
4. Port Seton Rotterdam	coal	158	106	105	59	29	457	—	145	8	Oct 1688 last Nov 1688	75
5. Elphinstoun Rotterdam	coal	166	154	176	50	25	571	—	215	8	1 April 1689 last June 1689	90
6. Wemyss Campvere	coal	142	106	161	35	5	449	—	80	5	mid July 1689 last Sept 1689	75
7. Port Seton London	coal	200	244	357	66	81	948	21	—	6	1 Nov 1689 mid April 1690	165
8. Methil London	coal	260	273	119	48	31 145**	731 145**	168	—	6	last July 1690 9 Dec 1690	130
TOTAL		1621	1429	1319	354	430	5153	396	492			

* As the dates if the vessel left or returned to port were not always provided, the length of each voyage is given as an estimate.

** Additional expenditure incurred as result of wreck.

In Holland the master purchased

Fresh fish		7	0
Green bread	7	4	4
Half barrel beer	2	0	4
Fresh fish		10	0
Beer	29	16	0

On the voyage to Norway the *George* put into Lerwick and purchased cows, oxen, 39 lbs of yeast, salt and a beef barrel. The animals would have been slaughtered by the crew as there is only one entry in the accounts of a payment to a man for slaughtering an ox. The crew would have undertaken this task as part of their normal duties and then salted the meat and put it into casks kept solely for this purpose. This meat would have been necessary to maintain them over the winter.

Beer and ale was a major item of expenditure as it was a recognised part of a seaman's diet; it was nutritious and to some extent prevented scurvy. Water was mainly used for cooking purposes. The beer and the water would have contained impurities and by the end of the voyage, the casks in which they were stored would have acquired an unpleasant flavour, requiring them to be dressed or cleaned at the end of each voyage. This task was not undertaken by the crew, for payment was made for this service. The total cost of food purchased for each voyage was reasonably constant with the exception of the second voyage, which lasted for 45 days. The cost for that voyage was practically the same as that purchased for a later voyage which lasted for 90 days. Large quantities of meat were purchased as well as biscuits and it is likely that there were sufficient supplies left over to be consumed on the following voyage. Meat was capable of being kept in good condition if kept in casks filled with brine but biscuits were subject to attack by weevils if stored for too long on the ship. (Davis, p. 366–7) Food was cooked on an open hearth which was installed prior to the ship embarking on the voyage to London in 1688 at a cost of £1 12s 0d. It could not have been well constructed as later in the same year the hearth was repaired at a cost of £4 8s 0d. The vent for the fire in the roof of the cabin would of necessity have had a small aperture, causing a very smoky atmosphere in bad weather. Two loads of peatss were purchased in Shetland in 1687. Due to the amount of smoke produced by peat when burned, the crew would have had no regrets when these loads were finished.

Wages

Table 3 gives a breakdown of the wages paid to the master, mate and seamen over the eight voyages made by the ship and it shows that there were no variations between the rates paid for the first three voyages if the length of the first voyage is taken into account. There is, however, a significant reduction in the rates paid for the fourth and fifth voyages. The ship made considerable losses on these two voyages, due perhaps to loss of markets and/or low freight rates and the crew would

*Table 3 Wages paid to master, mate and crew of the **George**, July 1687 – December 1690.*

Voyage	1		2		3		4		5		6		7		8	
	£	s	£	s	£	s	£	s	£	s	£	s	£	s	£	s
JAS Forrester	80	0	66	0	66	0	44	0	44	16	46	0	84	0	72	0
John Banks (Mate)	40	0	42	0	42	0	22	8	22	12						
Robt Couan	32	0	22	16	22	16			16	16						
Patrick Couan	32	0	22	16	22	16			16	16						
Wm Thomson	33	0	22	16	22	16	16	16			22	8				
Geo Pedin	18	0														
Mark Pedin	16	0														
Alex Mudie			22	16	22	16	16	16	16	16						
Jaspar Knouls			22	16	22	16	16	16								
Thom Turnbull							16	16	16	16	22	8	13	10		
John Lokert							16	16								
Murdie Mackloud							14	0	14	14	21	0	13	10		
Geo Cowan							10	0								
Adam Burnet (Mate)											30	4	60	0		
John Dycks													13	10		
Wm Forrester													15	0		
Ben Robertson															48	0
John Kerr (Mate)															60	0
David Shortis															33	0
James Shade															30	0
John Flukert															17	0

have had to accept a lower rate or stay onshore. However, though the rates were reduced the number of seamen increased from five to six. Ships of the period required much larger crews than later vessels of the same tonnage, for sails were larger requiring the efforts of all the crew to raise or lower them when wet and the tiller would have required two men to control it in stormy weather. In addition, without any mechanical aids the movement of cargoes in and out of the hold would also have involved the entire crew, so the additional members of the crew would have made a real difference.

It is therefore remarkable that on the sixth voyage the *George* undertook a voyage to Campvere which lasted approximately 75 days with only three seamen. The master and the mate would have had to undertake a considerable amount of extra duties on that voyage! On the seventh voyage the rate for the master and the mate was doubled although the rate for the seamen was reduced from £22 8s 0d to £13 10s 0d. The number of seamen had however been increased from three to four.

The rates paid to the seamen on the last voyage were very high in comparison to those paid on previous voyages. Whether this was due to the expectation of the ship making a profit, which it did on that voyage, or because there was a shortage of seamen due to impressment by the English Navy, is a matter for conjecture. It was apparently standard practice to engage both mates and crew at rates which did not take account of the probable length of the voyage. Traditionally, a master negotiated the rate of pay for a voyage with the owners and he was then responsible for engaging the crew and agreeing a rate for the voyage with them. Exception would be made for voyages which would likely be very long, such as the *George's* first voyage which lasted 260 days where the master was paid £80 0s 0d. His remuneration was reduced to £44 16s for the fifth voyage which lasted for 90 days. The important difference between these voyages was that the trading conditions between the summer of 1667 and the spring of 1689 were obviously very different and Forrester's bargaining power would have been much reduced. As freight rates would have been determined prior to the commencement of the voyage and the cost of operating the ship could have been ascertained by examining the costs of previous voyages, it is surprising that the voyage was undertaken when it would have been obvious that the voyage would result in a loss. It is, however, possible that the merchants who held shares in the ship were unaware of the losses incurred in earlier voyages.

England was in a state of war with France in 1689 and this would have led to an increased demand for seamen to serve in the Navy as well as closure of some overseas markets which normally would have been open to Scotland's merchants. The *George* apparently was unaffected by the war and continued to make voyages to Holland in 1689. It may be significant that in late 1689 and in 1690 her last voyages were made to London. On the seventh voyage an unspecified number (at least two) of the crew were pressed by a naval warship, leaving the *George* without sufficient seamen to continue the voyage. James Forrester would no doubt have made his position clear to the captain with the result that two members of the warship's crew were put on board the *George* to enable it to reach harbour. Forrester had to pay dearly for this assistance according to the following entry in the accounts:

Paid to the two men of war's men that did help us to London from Harwich after our own men being pressed... £14.8.0.

According to the accounts the ship completed the voyage with four men, all of whom were paid the same rate of pay, although two of their number (replacements engaged in London) only served for half of the voyage.

Of the ten who served for one voyage four were young seamen and four were the crew on the eighth and final voyage. These figures show that Forrester was able to retain men for several voyages. This is perhaps not surprising as the men would probably have been from the ports of Prestonpans and Port Seton and would have

Table 4   *Frequency of employment of seamen on the* **George.**

Employed for	Number so employed
5 voyages	1
4 voyages	5
3 voyages	1
2 voyages	0
1 voyage	<u>10</u>
	17

Table 5   *Costs of maintenance of the* **George,** *1687–1690.*

Element	Cost
Repairs to hull, rigging and sails	752
Purchase of equipment	259
Ballast	113
Cost of handling cargo and vessel in harbour	<u>195</u>
Total	£1,319

been known to him. The fact that many young men did not stay for more than one voyage was probably due to the hard life which they would have experienced on board a small ship. With no protection against the elements while working on deck without waterproof clothing, working conditions would have been very unpleasant during voyages made in the spring and late autumn.

Maintenance of the ship

Table 5 gives a breakdown of maintenance and operating costs for the *George* from 1687 to 1690, taken from Appendix III.

Regardless of the method of construction and the quality of materials used, seventeenth century ships had a major disadvantage that they were built of wood, a material that required considerable maintenance when used for ships' hulls. Timber is not a rigid material. It flexes and allows gaps between planking and joints, swells when water penetrates end or broken grains, shrinks when dry, and tends to rot if not appropriately treated. To avoid leakages shipwrights filled the gaps between planks by caulking them. This involved hammering in strands of old rope mixed with paint or oil called oakum. This apparently crude method was effective and when the planks were covered with tar the hull was reasonably, although never entirely, waterproof.

With the constant immersion and drying out of the timber and abrasion caused by rubbing against other hulls and quaysides, timber had to be replaced at frequent intervals. The disbursements of the *George* regularly included substantial payments to carpenters and blacksmiths for this work. Tar was purchased on several vaoyages and would have been used for general maintenance and to paint the hull after the ship was hauled up on to the shore for her annual careening, scraping and cleaning of the hull and replacement of damaged timber.

Sails and rigging were made of hemp, a material which was prone to stretching over a period and which therefore had to be repaired constantly and the standing rigging had to be adjusted because it stretched, unlike the standing rigging of later ships which was made of iron and required little maintenance. Standing rigging was under constant strain and if too much movement was allowed the ship was liable to lose masts in bad weather.

The work on maintaining the ship in good repair did not involve a great deal of expenditure when compared to the total cost of running the ship, as much of the work was carried out by the crew. A substantial part of the cost of maintenance was incurred by paying skilled men, who would have been employed when the ship was in harbour, although a carpenter was carried as a member of the crew for one voyage.

At different times throughout the period, various items of equipment such as hawsers, sails, and anchors, which were very expensive, and minor items such as scrapers and lanterns, were purchased. For the *George*, a relatively small ship spending a considerable period in port during the winter, maintenance costs formed a much smaller proportion (26%) of total costs than was incurred by large ocean-going ships.

The *George* would have carried ballast consisting of large stones at all times and this would have been supplemented by loose ballast which would have been required in order to keep the ship stable after the cargo had been unloaded. Sailing ships when empty rode high in the water and would have been at the mercy of high wind unless ballast, amounting in the case of the *George* to 30–40 tons, was carried. The nature of the ballast taken on board depended upon what was available at the port where the cargo was discharged; it could be shingle or sand gathered from a beach or dragged from the bed of a river. Sand was perhaps more readily available but it clogged the pump so would have been taken only as a last resort. Taking ballast on board was a laborious and time consuming task and the loose material had to be stowed correctly to avoid it moving in a storm; partitions were erected in the hold to prevent this.

Offloading ballast at the end of a voyage presented the master with a problem since the harbour authorities did not want the harbour's entrance or the harbours themselves to be filled with rubble. As early as 1561 the Town Council of Aberdeen imposed a fine of 40 shillings on any ship casting out ballast within the flood mark (L.B. Taylor p. 7). Although ballast would have been required on every voyage (as the *George* only obtained one cargo when returning to Scotland) the accounts record only three payments for discharging ballast, so James Forrester would have got rid of it in deep water when the weather was calm. The charges were £2 and £3.6s, high enough for a master to avoid payment when the opportunity arose. Harbour authorities allocated areas for dumping of ballast; areas which would eventually be reclaimed from the sea. There are many examples of astute masters bringing back as ballast cargoes such as roof tiles from Holland and large stones which could be used as building material. The harbour authorities of Tyneside enforced regulations for dealing with ballast for this was a major problem with so many ships dumping their ballast when entering the river. A Tyneside ship, having taken a cargo of coal to London, would have had to pay a shilling per ton for ballast and sixpence for putting it on board. The ship would then be charged another shilling for putting the ballast ashore (Finch p. 163).

Moving cargo in and out of the hold of ships was very hard work if the ship was not lying at a quayside and the accounts for seven of the eight voyages record payments to men to carry out this work which was apparently seen as labour in addition to the crew's work as seamen. The term 'liver' was used to describe the work of unloading cargo.

The amounts paid for this work varied widely and included the provision of meat or food and drink. As carpenters were engaged in this work they would have been required to carry out repairs and build bulkheads in order to prevent the cargo shifting in heavy weather. One other task which they might have had to do was the setting up of spars or derricks for the lifting of cargo from the quay or lighters into the hold of the ship. The fact that Forrester fed the people involved in loading the cargo, a hard and dirty job, showed that it was treated to some extent as a community activity involving a number of the inhabitants of Port Seton. Examples of these payments involving the consumption of meat and drink were as follows:

	£	s	d	£	s	d
Voyage No 2. Destination London. Cargo Salt						
Meat & drink to my men and boys in time of livering	6	0	0			
Drink to my men in time of loading	1	9	6			
Meat & drink to the carpenters and boys in time of						
lying in the harbour	30	0	0	37	9	6
Voyage No 7. Destination London. Cargo Coal						
Meat & drink to the carpenters and boys				40	0	0

Harbour charges

A shipmaster wishing to load or unload a cargo at a port on the eastern seaboard of Scotland in the seventeenth century would have experienced considerable difficulty unless the port provided a safe anchorage and a reasonable amount of shelter. Towns with these features were Leith, Bo'ness, Kirkcaldy, Dundee, Montrose, Aberdeen and Inverness, all of which had been important trading centres since medieval times. There were a number of small harbours in the Firth of Forth such as Bo'ness, Port Seton and Prestonpans which were suitable for ships of the same size as the *George*. As maritime trade developed in the sixteenth and seventeenth centuries and ships increased in size and in number, all the large ports attempted to increase the protection to ships lying off the shore by building breakwaters and quays which allowed ships to discharge cargoes without the use of lighters. The port records of both Leith and Aberdeen show that considerable expenditure was incurred in order to provide a safe haven with facilities such as quays for loading and unloading cargoes. The small natural harbours were also developed by wealthy landowners wishing to export the produce of their areas, such as coal, salt and grain. These facilities were mainly limited to the construction of two piers which had a limited capability for taking ships of a reasonable size. The majority of ships of that period engaged in exporting goods to the Continent and England were between 50 and 100 tons so the facilities were usually adequate for the purpose of the trade carried out by the Forth ports.

Building an underwater structure strong enough to withstand the force of the sea was often a question of trial and error, and many of the original quays were rebuilt several times because there were very few men in the country capable of doing this work. The maintenance of these harbour defences required considerable expenditure on a regular basis and charges were levied by burghs and landowners for the use of their harbours. Burghs wishing to levy these charges were required to petition the Convention of Royal Burghs 'to impetrat at our Soverane Lord' in the form of a petition laid before Parliament in which they craved the right to raise funds by some form of taxation. Aberdeen requested the Convention to seek a levy in 1596 and this was granted (L.B. Taylor p. 3). The scale of charges laid down and later amended was similar to that used by the Port of Leith and it is likely it was also used by other east coast ports. The ability to make charges meant that burghs then had the resources to enable them to carry out maintenance and improvement work on a regular basis.

The services provided to the *George* and the payments made by the ship when entering and leaving harbours in Scotland, London and Rotterdam were of a similar nature. However the scale of charges levied outside Scotland were considerably greater due to the larger number of vessels using the port requiring a greater range of facilities and more port employees. The payment for anchorage for ships of 60 tons and over in Leith and Aberdeen was £1 3s 4d. This payment would have been made by ships lying in sheltered water outside the harbour waiting their turn to load and unload their cargoes at the quays. When a vessel was able to dock at a quay it would have been charged for that facility, called berthage in some ports and wharf-age in others. Plankage was the term used to describe the payment made to Leith Porters Society for the use of gangplanks connecting the ship to the quay.

There were very few lights or beacons positioned round the coasts of Scotland and England in the seventeenth century. Leith provided a light on the Island of May and lights were provided at harbour mouths of major ports such as London and Rotterdam. In his summary statement at the end of his accounts, James Forrester records a payment of £30 for the Light of May for eight voyages at £3 15s per voyage. The Privy Council in 1635 had granted a patent to John Cunningham and James Maxwell to collect dues of 4s per ton on foreign ships and 2s on Scottish ships for the building and upkeep of the light. The *George* had a burthen of 40 tuns according to the charge for Adair's services but this charge was based for some reason on a ship of 37½ tuns. Payment of the light dues was obviously done as and when the master decided payment was due, unlike payment of harbour and custom dues. No doubt the seafaring community of the Firth appreciated the benefit of the light and as responsible men paid their dues, albeit somewhat late. The Town Council of Aberdeen erected on St Ninian's Chapel on the Castlehill 'ane gryt bowat or lamp quhair the same was obefoir … with thre gryt flammand lychts' (Clark p. 11). These aids to mariners would have been essential in large ports such as London and Rotterdam and would have required considerable maintenance. This was reflected in the high charges for this service, £6 1s by London and £6 14s by Rotterdam. Buoyage was paid on two occasions when the ship was in Rotterdam which, being a very busy port, would always have ships tied to buoys while waiting their turn to discharge their cargoes at the quays. Because these buoys were in constant usage and subject to considerable strain, the cables attaching them to the river bed would have been subject to regular inspections and replacements. Last money was paid at Rotterdam and as a last is a unit of measurement equivalent to two tons it would have been based on the weight of the cargo. It was only paid once so it may have been charged to cover expenditure on a specific project for that port. Last money was levied by Aberdeen on cargoes carried by foreigners as an additional source of revenue.

Pilot fees were paid on five occasions: Shetland £2 18s, Rotterdam £28 12s 4d and £4 4s 8d, from Campvere to Rotterdam £12 13s and Methil in Fife, where the entry reads: 'Payment to the Bucker for pilotage out and in to the Methill £3.0.0'. Forrester would not have required the services of a pilot in the Lothian ports which with the exception of Leith were small, and no doubt easy to enter. Methil was also a small port and may have had a difficult entrance to the harbour. The pilot was a 'bucker' or an inhabitant of Buckhaven, a neighbouring port, and as the charge for pilotage was high it would have been paid with ill grace. Rotterdam would not have been an easy port to enter or leave because of the number of ships using it and the authorities would have ensured an efficient system for controlling ships entering and leaving the port. The high port charges for Rotterdam were of little importance to merchants as they knew that cargoes would have a ready market in this a major European trading centre and cargoes would have been unloaded without unreasonable delay. The short time taken on the two voyages to Rotterdam reveal the effectiveness of the port administration.

The *George* must have lost an anchor and cable in a deep part of the river, and had to pay for its recovery. The entry reads: '*To the pilots for getting my cable and anchor again at the Pit…£14.*' From the entry it can be assumed that this was not the first occasion upon which recovery had proven necessary.

All vessels, large or small, would have been liable for harbour dues and these would have been paid with ill grace by the masters, making the task of extracting money from them an onerous one in a large port.

The duties of the shore dues tacksman of Leith in 1734 are given below (Mowat p. 250–51) and show that he was responsible for collecting beaconage and anchorage and also for the dues on the amount and the nature of the cargo unloaded. Aberdeen charged a duty of so much a tun of wine, grain and salt. Leith would have had its own scale of charges for the various commodities which were imported. The dues to be paid on these cargoes would have been the liability of the merchant importing the goods and would not have been charged against the ship. Tacksmen did not have an easy role and in a large and busy harbour would have to work very hard to avoid the penalty for the loss of revenue given in the second paragraph of his list of duties.

The duties of the collector of shore dues

You are to enter in this Register all vessels which have come into the Harbour of Leith since Martinmas 1734. Excepting such Ferry Boats as belong to Burntisland, Kinghorn and Kirkcaldy, coming from these places without goods and having only passengers on board.

You are to take particular care, how soon any vessel arrives to enter the true date, the master's and merchant's names, and places from which it comes. And immediately when livered [unloaded] (or sooner if you can know it with any certainty) you are to note the true qualities and quantities of the cargo, and whether the same is free or unfree. You are to take special care that all ships Masters and others liable, pay their Beaconage and Anchorage before they are quite livered, or at least immediately thereafter, for if you allow them to sail without paying, you are hereby certified it shall be charged on you, and stopped out of your salary.

All vessels from London, Newcastle or Holland or from the North Country with fish, oil, butter, skins etc, collected at the plank end, are to be accounted for by you within 8 days after they are fully livered. Therefore you are to allow none, whether factors or others, to carry their goods from off the Shore till you are satisfied. If you do, it shall be on your own account and charged on you as above.

And if any person without paying or consigning to the full extent of the dues (and you'll take care to require no more than the table allows) pretend to carry off their goods, you are to hipotheque [take in pledge] and secure such a quantity thereof as shall be sufficient for our payment. For which goods you are to offer your receipt, mentioning their being hypothecated by you for their refusal of the payment of the Shore Dues etc.

You are also to discharge the Workmen and others from assisting in carrying off said goods, as directed in your printed Table, signed by the Treasurer, precept by the Admiral of Leith [one of the Bailies] etc. You'll also notice the clause in said Table whereby you are authorised to exact the whole merk per tun if the goods imported shall be foreign, and full Shore Dues, whether foreign or inland, from such persons as shall refuse to pay their just dues.

You are [to] make out, sum up and deliver over to us weekly your account of cash received, distinguishing what is proper to last year from this.

Sundry charges

On a voyage to Rotterdam in 1689, payment of £43 18s 4d was paid for convoy money. This was apparently the ship's share of the charges imposed by the English Navy. Scotland did not have ships at this time capable of providing adequate protection for her merchant ships trading in the North Sea. England had just declared war against the French in August of that year and action by French naval vessels and privateers on Scots and English merchantmen would have been expected. A voyage later that year to Campvere also incurred a charge for convoy money but this time the charge was only £3 10s.

England was concerned that the French would land men in the west of Scotland knowing that there were many Jacobite sympathisers amongst the population, and naval ships constantly patrolled these waters. Because of their need of experienced men, the Navy impressed Scots seamen disregarding the fact that they required approval from the King before doing so. Although this high-handed action caused considerable friction between the two countries, it was clear from the payments made for convoy money that Scots found it necessary to use the service of the Navy (E.J. Graham p. 96).

On the same voyage James Forrester also paid £20 4s 'for my protection' and this payment, it is assumed, meant that the crew were protected from being pressed into the service of the Royal Navy, which was short of men during a period of war. An extract from the kind of protection which would have been granted to Forrester is given below (Grant p. 67–8). The document makes no mention of a charge to be paid.

The George of Port Seton

Edinburgh. 13th February, 1690

Follows the tenor of the protection [to a Scots ship] granted in the terms of the proclamation of Council made anent levying of seamen:

The Lords of his Majesty's Privy Council, considering that his Majesty by his royal letter of the date at Kensington, the fourth day of January last bypast, 1690, hath recommended to the said Lords to find out a way for raising a competent number of Scots seamen for his service, being resolved that Scotsmen, if prisoners, shall be equally relieved with the English, and that Scots trading ships shall have protection on board for preventing their men being pressed; and that the said Lords of Privy Council, by their proclamation of the date the tenth day of the said month of January last bypast, have appointed the magistrates of the several maritime burghs, royal and other sea towns to cause beat drums and levy seamen to serving in their Majesties' fleet in the way and manner and on the conditions particularly expressed in the said proclamation, by which they have promised to such who shall affectionately show their forwardness on that occasion that they shall have particular protections on board each one of their ships given them to be free of any pressure here or by any of their Majesties' men-of-war in any of their ports: and the Council understanding that, besides the number of thirty-four seamen who voluntarily listed themselves and are presently in their Majesties' actual service, belonging to the town of Dundee, that the magistrates of that burgh have presently taken on eleven other volunteer seamen and have paid them their levy money and maintenance and have sent up a list of all the other seamen within their bounds, that the Council may give further directions anent them:

Therefore they by virtue of the power and warrant granted to them and in the terms of the former proclamation of Council, hereby grant protection to Robert Kinloch, skipper and master of the good ship called the Rachell of Dundee, and to the seamen afternamed aboard the same, to wit, William Oliphant, Andrew Rutherford, Thomas Gibsone, John Gibsone, and John Knoxs, mariners in Dundee, with a boy, presently bound for London upon the account of James Fletcher, present provost of Dundee, or any other seamen to the number of five who afterwards shall sail, the said ship to be free from any pressure in this kingdom or from any pressure from any of his Majesty's men-of-war, or in any of their Majesties' ports: And they do hereby request all the commanders of their Majesties' men-of-war, press masters and all other officers, civil and military, and other whom it shall or may concern, to suffer and permit the said ship, with her loading and ship's crew, freely and quietly to sail from the port of Dundee to London or any where else, and to return again to any port within this kingdom or to any other port belonging to their Majesties or any in alliance with them without any let, trouble or molestation whatsoever, they behaving and demeaning themselves according to their duty and their allegiance to their Majesties and their royal authority. And they declare that this protection shall only continue and endure for the space of one year after the date hereof. Signed by warrant and at command of the Lords of his Majesty's Privy Council, by William, Earl of Crafurd, elected president of Council in absence of their president, and sealed with the cachet of Council at Edinburgh, the day and year aforesaid, and of their Majesties' reign the first year.

CRAFURD, I.P.D.S. Con

James Forrester paid the sum of £9 'for my Gold Penny ticket' (a thanks offering for safe return from a dangerous voyage) before setting off on a voyage to Norway. He did so presumably because he knew that the voyage would be a long one, as it involved going round Scotland to Greenock, then to Orkney, Shetland and Norway. The voyage, which lasted from June 1687 to March 1688, was not without risk. It is noteworthy that the payment was not on a personal basis from James Forrester, shipmaster, but was included as part of the expenditure incurred on the voyage and perhaps it could be described as insurance. The gold penny had another function in some parts of Scotland, that of dues collected on all ships built or sold and the revenue would have been retained by the Admiral Depute for the area, who would be a prominent local landowner or the Provost of a coastal burgh. In Aberdeen, shipmasters paid the gold penny to guildry funds, thus ensuring that those who survived a life at sea benefited from these funds in their old age.

In addition to the recognised duties of a shipmaster, James Forrester undertook the task of procuring cargoes and passengers. The following entries in the accounts show that substantial sums of money were incurred in so doing.

Voyage		£
1	My own expenses to Greenock from Seton to get my freight and for my horse hire	12
1	My extraordinary expenses in terms of the voyage	12
2	For my extraordinary expenses in procuring passengers and goods	12
3	For my extraordinary expenses in procuring passengers and goods	6
7	My extraordinary expenses procuring goods and passengers	18
7	Expenses in seeking my freight	6
8	My extraordinary expenses	12

The first item involved going across Scotland on horseback to Greenock, and with roads clearly in poor condition it must have been a long and painful journey for a seaman. It is notable that Forrester did not specify the nature of the expenditure incurred, and that the sums were rounded up. It is likely that he had to seek out people who would provide him with information on passengers and cargoes that might be taken and that much of that expenditure would have been on food and drink as well as the payment for information provided. There would have been no receipts to justify these payments! Whatever methods were employed, the extraordinary expenses were entirely justified for he succeeded in obtaining income well in excess of his expenditure. Large cargoes, however, could only be obtained by establishing relationships with Edinburgh merchants and this task would have been beyond the ability of a shipmaster from a small port such as Port Seton.

On four voyage payment was made 'for putting my bill in exchange'. These payments, it is assumed, must have been the commission that Forrester had to pay for a Bill of Exchange, in order that he could obtain money for food and materials. It is curious that there are no other entries in the acounts relating to the interest payable on these bills. One reason why Forrester may have wanted to obtain bills of exchange was that he was trading on his own account and required money to purchase goods (although this assumption has no supporting evidence).

Customs charges

As a result of the report made in 1656 by Thomas Tucker on the state of the customs service in Scotland, more effective organisation was instituted which ensured that a much higher proportion of duty would be collected on imports and exports. Scotland was divided into Precincts which covered the greater part of the east coast, Dumfries, Ayrshire, the Firth of Clyde and the border with England, with each Precinct having a head port where the office of the collector and his staff was situated. In 1656 the head ports were Leith, Bo'ness, Dundee, Aberdeen, Burntisland, Inverness, Ayr and Glasgow. By the 1680s, as a result of increased overseas trade, additional Precincts were established, with collectors being based at Prestonpans, Montrose, Port Glasgow, Irvine and Port Patrick. The procedures to be followed by a merchant or shipmaster taking goods out of or into the country were set out explicitly in *Rules, Orders and Instructions for Custom Officers made by the Commissioners of Customs and Excise 1656*.

As was required, James Forrester duly reported the arrival or impending departure of his ship to the customs office of the port and had to pay the requisite fee. This charge was on occasions included with other costs so it is not possible to state the amount of the reporting fee. It varied from £1 8s 0d to £3 7s 0d with the charges paid in London and Fraserburgh being the highest. The charge was paid on every voyage except that from Port Seton to Rotterdam in 1688. The only entry for payment to Custom officials on that voyage is for '*writing my passport £1 16s*' and '*to the waiters for subscribing my passport £0 14s 0d*'. As it was the duty of waiters to check the loading and unloading of cargo, it could be assumed that the entries on the passport were recorded in a custom outport book.

On two occasions Forrester paid charges to customs 'For my sufferance £0 12s 0d'. This term referred to the permission given by customs to a master to ship or discharge cargoes which have already paid excise duty at a specific port. Figure 19 shows a copy of this document.

The form of a Permit, or Sufferance.

Leith Excise.

IN the Sarah of Brunt-Iſland, Anthony Lilburn Maſter, pro Inverneſſe,

Michael Craig Retailer,

Two Hogſheads of French Wines
but not to be Exported without further order.
Dated the day of
A. B. Collector. C. D. Cheque.

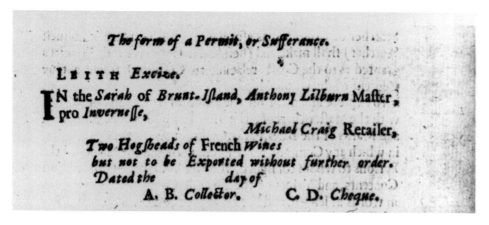

Figure 19 Part of the form of sufferance. Reproduced by permission of the Trustees of the National Library of Scotland.

According to the *Rules, Orders and Instructions*, goods could not be shipped from port to port until a 'cocket' had been passed which was a legal document certifying that a cargo had been recorded in customs registers and that duty had been paid. The amounts paid by the *George* for the cocket varied. The second and third voyages to London with a cargo of coal incurred £12 14*s* and £11 8*s* respectively and on the seventh voyage, also to London with coal, £4 16*s* 0*d* was paid to get the documentation.

The *Rules* state that the collector of the Precinct would issue cockets stating that security had been given or duties paid for a particular cargo which was to be exported. A charge of one pound Scots was paid at Port Seton when the ship left for Rotterdam in 1688 with a cargo of coal. Coastwise voyages apparently required more careful scrutiny by customs officials and therefore more documentation than overseas voyages. Figure 20 shows the form of a cocket. The *Rules* used the term 'Cocquet' although cocket was the description in use since the fifteenth century.

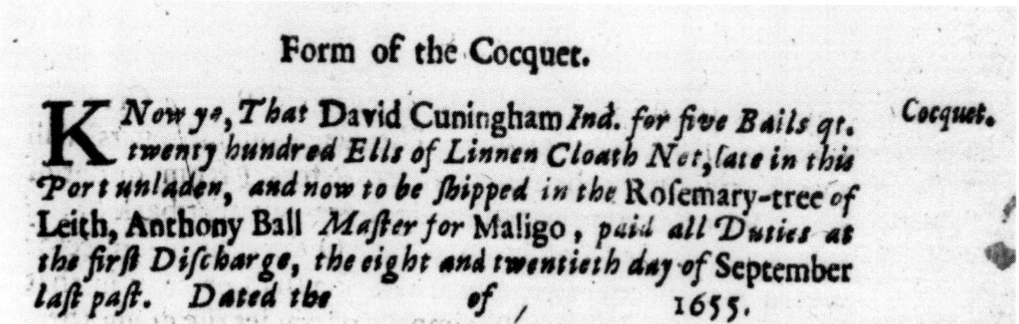

Form of the Cocquet.

KNow ye, That David Cuningham Ind. for five Bails qt. twenty hundred Ells of Linnen Cloath Net, late in this Port unladen, and now to be ſhipped in the Roſemary-tree of Leith, Anthony Ball Maſter for Maligo, paid all Duties at the firſt Diſcharge, the eight and twentieth day of September laſt paſt. Dated the of 1655. Cocquet.

Figure 20 The form of coquet. Reproduced by permission of the Trustees of the National Library of Scotland.

The Last voyage of the *George*

In April 1690 the *George* returned to Port Seton after a voyage to London which had lasted five months. The ship had spent the greater part of the time lying in the lower reaches of the Thames unable to leave the safety of the river because of bad weather. The ship was obviously in need of repairs, for the first entry in the disbursement record for her next voyage was in payment to: '*Mrs Tait for meat and drink to my men, boys and carpenters from 8 April to last July 1690 £29 13s 0d.*' The second and third entries were for work done by '*David Durie for carpenter work £23 16s 0d*' and '*Alexander Sands for supply of pitch & tar £15 0s 0d.*'

The length of time that the men, boys and carpenters were employed showed that the ship required considerable work to be done on her hull, sails and rigging before James Forrester considered her ready to go to sea. The ship had a charter to take a cargo of great coal from Methil to London and four men were employed at a cost of £8 8s 0d to take the ship across to Fife. In Methil he paid £20 18s 0d for 'meat and drink to my men and boys there for their services in loading the ship with coal,' a dirty, hard and thirsty job regardless whether the cargo had to be loaded from a quay or a beach. The payment to four men to sail the ship to Fife is odd in the light of the references to payment to 'his men' both in Port Seton and Methil who, it must be assumed, were members of the crew and therefore capable of sailing the ship to Methil.

While in London he bought 114 lbs of rope for £18 12s and paid £30 16s for beer and wharfage, an odd combination. In addition, food was purchased for the crew and the passengers who apparently were going to get better food than the crew. It was likely that the pasengers and crew ate at different times, with the crew getting the basic fare. The crew presumably slept in the hold for there was limited accommodation available in the cabin. On the homeward voyage the *George* anchored off Yarmouth, where beef was purchased. After leaving this port the ship ran into stormy weather and was driven ashore at Scarborough.

The entries in the accounts of the ship relating to the wreck are as follows:

	£
To the Customhouse at Scarborough for the entry of the wreck	18
My mens diet at Scarborough	3
To my men to carry them home	12
For saving the rigging and carrying it from the wreck to Scarborough	96
Paid at the Customhouse at Scarborough per receipt	18
	£147

As there was at that time no system for registering vessels with customs, there would not appear to be any reason for recording the wreck, nor why there should be two payments of £18. One explanation for this payment to customs could be that it was payment for dues on the cargo which may have been damaged by seawater and a nominal sum charged. The master was still responsible for the crew even though the *George* was wrecked, and had to pay for their welfare when rescued and for their transport back to Scotland. The accounts also show that the men received their wages which may have been only a proportion of the sums agreed because the voyage was not completed.

Details of the income obtained from the cargo taken to London on the last voyage and the money received from the goods recovered from the wrecked ship are the last entries in the account book and are given below.

For upward freight to London by bulk, received	£564
For the hold and rigging of the wreck when she was lost, received	£480
	£1,044

Passengers were carried on the voyage from London to Scotland (as food was prepared for them) but there is no entry of a fare being paid. It is thus conjecture whether their fares were returned to them or retained by Forrester (for passengers would have paid at the start of the voyage).

The vessel would appear to have been driven ashore at a point from which it was possible to board the ship and remove the cargo and equipment. The term 'rigging' refers to sails and rope and 'hold' means the cargo therein, which was being taken back to Scotland. Sails and rope would have found a ready market in a busy port such as Scarborough. The price obtained for the cargo would have depended on the nature of the goods and, as they came from London, they would no doubt also have found a market in any part of the country.

As master, James Forrester would have been responsible for removing as much cargo, sails and rigging as possible from the *George* and, in addition, for the transportation of these salvaged items to Scarborough. The work of removing the rigging from the wreck must have involved labour other than the crew, for he had to pay the sum of £96 for its removal and transportation. It would not have been a pleasant task for a master to supervise the dismantling of his ship, however, in view of the substantial sums received, it was a very necessary one. When he obtained the proceeds from the sale, and paid customs the sums due to them, James Forrester would then have had to find a passage on a ship going to Scotland, perhaps not a difficult task in view of the number of ships which were engaged in the coastal trade at that time. His passage home was obtained apparently without cost as there is no record of it in the accounts.

Losses and some profit

A summary of the trading ventures of the *George* over nine voyages shows that the ship made a net loss of £332 if the proceeds of the wreck are taken into account. This is somewhat surprising as the ship did not stay long in any port and, in comparison with the majority of other ships from Firth of Forth ports, the *George* was one of the few ships making two to three voyages per annum. The owners of the ship are not known, so it is not possible to ascertain whether they were coal and/or salt producers using the ship to transport their products and expecting to meet any loss incurred in operating the ship out of profits from the sale of their goods. Given that the ship was in port for a comparatively short period, this would indicate that the suppliers of coal and salt had agents both in London and Holland capable of obtaining customers for these commodities. Arrangements to obtain customers for cargoes such as coal and salt would have been comparatively straightforward, unlike cargoes of mixed goods.

Investors in ships usually took shares in more than one vessel so as to spread the risk, for shipowning was a precarious venture in those days, with possible losses through bad weather, war and actions of privateers.

The records relating to a case which came before the Admiralty Court in 1710 involving a ship called the *George of Prestonpans* lists the following owners (AC 9/ 381).

Wm. PANTON, Writer to the Signet
BARBARA GUTHRIE, Wife
AND. SUTHERLAND, Writer to the Signet
THO. WILSON, Cooper, Leith
MARION WILKIE, Wife
EARL OF WINTON
Wm. ROBERSON, Clerk of Session
JN. MATHIE, Skipper, Prestonpans
JA. GIBSON, Mariner, Prestonpans
ALEXR. CARSTAIRS, Merchant, Rotterdam
ALRXR. WINEBERG, Rope Maker, Rotterdam
THO. CRAWFORD, Merchant, Rotterdam
Mr ROBERT FORBES

Some of those listed would have been fellow townsmen who would have known the ship and her master and have considered them both to be a sound investment. This would certainly apply to Thomas Wilson, the cooper in Leith. The two Scots who were merchants in Rotterdam would have had regular correspondence and personal contacts with Scotland and would have been well informed about the state of trade, the quality of the ship, and, just as relevant, the ability of her master. (The terms skipper, mariner and master appear to be interchangeable and apparently did not relate to the size of the vessel.)

With large ships which had several owners, one shareholder, not always the one with the largest share, usually acted as manager, arranging for cargoes with factors and giving instructions to the master on how and where these cargoes would be collected and delivered. In smaller ships the master would have been responsible for obtaining cargoes and dealing with factors, harbour authorities and customs. Some merchants would have had shares in more than one vessel and thereby gained valuable information on the state of overseas markets and European shipping. The Earl of Winton is recorded as a shareholder of two ships although the number of shares held by him is not given. As the Earl owned coal mines and salt pans, he would have found it very much in his interest to have shares in vessels since he would have been able to arrange for the ships to be available to carry his cargoes of salt and coal. The accounts record that the cargoes of coal carried on the second and third voyages were for the 'Noble Earl of Winton'. The practice of owning shares in ships was not confined to merchants and tradesmen in Edinburgh and Leith, for the Admiralty Court Records show that the system was widely adopted by merchants of other Scottish burghs. At that time there was no legal limit to the number of people allowed to take shares in a ship and an examination of shareholders named in a number of cases ranged from two to nineteen.

The only known contemporary record of trading is that of James Kerr, an Edinburgh merchant, whose ledgers for the period 1688–90 give details of his trading both in goods and maritime ventures. Kerr made substantial overall profits on these voyages in addition to the profits made on other parts of his business. The ledgers do not provide sufficient details of the voyages in which he had an interest to be able to ascertain whether the ship had a cargo on the outward and inward voyages. As a merchant Kerr would have had adequate knowledge of cargoes to be obtained both in Scotland, England and Holland, and this would have placed him in a favourable position to ensure that his ship carried some freight on homeward voyages (NAS RH 9/1 258–260). Certainly Kerr would have been better placed to ensure that cargoes were obtained than the owners of the *George*, who relied on James Forrester to obtain cargoes for the return voyages. As custom records show, there was a large number of ships bringing cargoes into the Prestonpans Precinct and a similar position would have applied to Leith because of its size and importance.

Evidence that there was a considerable number of merchants in Edinburgh who were engaged in trading with other parts of Scotland, England and the Continent during the latter part of the sixteenth century is given in an article by M.H.B. Sanderson which summarized the testaments of 205 merchants for the period 1570 to 1603. The majority of these men left estates which were comparatively small from £500 to £3000 sterling and whose activities would have been restricted mainly to inland towns and coastal trade with east coast ports with some participation in overseas trade.

As in every other trading port there were wealthy merchants who were engaged in various activities such as money lending, part-ownership of vessels, maintaining stocks of merchandise and landowning in addition to carrying out extensive trade with the Continent and England. Whilst these men came from different social backgrounds they had of necessity extensive commercial relationships with other merchants in major ports throughout Scotland.

When a ship was required to transport goods it was the general practice to charter a ship, for only a few of the merchants were part-owners of ships. Because of the risk in transporting cargoes it was the practice for merchants to take shares in large cargoes and, if the merchandise was valuable, to have it carried in more than one ship. There is evidence in the testaments that these merchants made extensive use of the services of factors who resided in various ports in France, Holland, Denmark, Poland and in Danzig. These agents would arrange to sell or store cargoes and remit the proceeds back to Scotland or purchase goods which would form the cargoes for the return journey (Cowan and Shaw, pp. 182–199).

It is obvious that the owners of the *George* did not use the services of factors because, out of six voyages to London and Rotterdam, only one resulted in a substantial amount of freight on the homeward voyage. It is improbable that the first voyage to Norway produced a cargo of timber as this commodity was normally carried on Norwegian ships. The accounts record that the cargoes carried on the return voyage were limited to eggs, sundry goods and passengers. There was, however, one item of cargo carried on the second voyage which resulted in a substantial freight charge and the entry in the accounts reads *'For Goffords Corps £144 0s 0d'*. This would appear to be a very substantial sum to pay to transport a body from London to Scotland. As a pound Scots was worth one twelfth of a pound sterling the amount paid to Forrester may not have meant very much to the late Gofford's representatives in London. It is not possible to state who Gofford was although it is very likely he was a Scot from a well-to-do family willing to pay to have his body buried in his native country. The circumstances of his death and why James Forrester agreed to transport the body in his ship would make an interesting story if known.

There was, however, a significant increase in the value of cargo taken on the seventh voyage from London and, from the record of money received from the recovery of the wreck of the *George*, it would appear that the ship was also carrying a cargo of some value on its last voyage. It was likely that the owners had arranged charters for the ship on her return voyage with Edinburgh merchants for the last two voyages. The customs outport record for the Port of Leith provides details of this cargo carried on the seventh voyage. The entries cover five pages and show in detail the goods which were imported. There were 15 merchants and two lairds involved in this cargo which covered a wide variety of goods: lemons, oranges, lampblock, oil, powder horns, cloth, looking glasses, whiting, iron work, gingerbread, leather, tin, to name only a few (NAS E 72/15/45). Before a cargo could have been purchased, various merchants would have approached a factor or factors, presumably in Edinburgh, to make their requirements known. Prior to this, the owners of the *George* would have met with the factors and informed them that they had a ship available for charter. The factors would have arranged with their agents in London to supply these goods and charter the ships to carry the goods.

Whatever the profits made on the transporting of coal and salt, it would have made commercial sense to endeavour to supplement the efforts made by James Forrester to obtain freight. As the records show, cargoes were available, and the owners had a good sound ship and a competent master. Without further information on profits earned on the cargoes of salt and coal, and the names of the individual owners of the ship and her cargo, it is not possible to determine the reasons why the ship was apparently allowed to operate at a loss for such a long period.

On the last page of the disbursements, James Forrester set out a summary of the profits and losses made on each voyage, together with a list of payments incurred by him in the execution of his duties as master, totalling £116. This sum of £116, together with net loss of £332, giving a total of £448, was the amount due to Forrester by the owners over the period covered by these nine voyages. This is a very unusual statement for it was normal practice for accounts to be submitted by a master at the end of each voyage, and for him to pay any surplus to the owners or to be reimbursed if a loss was incurred. It is apparent from this statement that the master was either meeting the losses and/or retaining the profits made on each voyage. As the ship operated at a loss for most of her life, this required Forrester to

TABLE 6 *Income obtained from freights carried by the* **George.**

VOYAGES		INCOME			
		OUTWARD £	INWARD £	TOTAL £	EXPENDITURE £
1 Cockenzie	London	906	—	906	744
2 Port Seton	London	438	228	666	621
3 Port Seton	London	343	92	435	487
4 Port Seton	Rotterdam	303	9	312	457
5 Elphinstoune	Rotterdam	310	46	356	571
6 Wemyss	Campvere	363	6	369	449
7 Port Seton	London	626	343	969	948
8 Methil	London	564	—	564	876
		3853	724	4577	5153
Loss incurred on an earlier voyage					236
Proceeds from the wreck				480	
				5057	
Net loss				332	
				£5389	5389

NOTE: There is an arithmetical error of £10 in the records which overstates the total of expenditure. The correct net loss was £322.

finance these operations from his own resources. As the statement makes the un-named owners responsible for all the losses, it follows that Forrester was not a shareholder. This makes his financing of the operation of the ship for such a long period even more remarkable. There are no records of Leith Baillie Court in exist-ence to show whether Forrester took action against the owners to that court in 1691 in order to obtain the monies due to him. The fact that the book containing the records of disbursements of the *George* was used by the Clerk to the Leith Baillie Court in 1747 could mean it was used as evidence in an earlier court case.

If one of the owners of the ship had been the Earl of Winton, it would not have been an easy matter for the master of the *George* to approach him and request that he meet his share of the losses incurred either during the period of the nine voyages or after the wreck. As the Earl owned salt pans and mines in the vicinity of Port Seton and the ship carried five cargoes of these commodities from that port, it is very likely that they were carried on behalf of the Earl. The Earl may well have found it expedient to be a shareholder in the ship because he would have had some say in its availability to carry his cargoes. This is however conjecture, and the Earl may have had no connection with the ship, and the owners could well have consisted of the usual mixture of Leith and Port Seton men.

It was not an unusual occurrence apparently for owners to avoid contributing towards their share of the losses. A number of cases involving non-payment are recorded in Admiralty Court records during this period. A summary of a case before the Admiralty Court in December 1691 concerns an Alexander Pratt, skipper of Bo'ness, master and owner of the *Mary of Bo'ness*. Pratt was master for several years and had been unable to get three of the owners to pay their share of ex-penses. As a result he had to borrow £120 sterling on a Bottomry bond from a London merchant and now applied for the ship to be rouped so that he could clear his debts. The court upheld his right to sell the ship (AC 7/9 5 Dec 1691).

Chapter Three

Coal, salt and sundry goods

The trade conducted by the ports of the Lothians and south-east Fife during the period 1685–95 constituted some three-quarters of the country's trade with the Continent and England, and made an essential contribution to the economy. In comparison with well-developed countries such as Holland and England, Scotland was a very small producer of goods such as coal, salt, hides and plaiding. That Scottish merchants were able to find markets for these goods showed that they had considerable commercial enterprise, but also reflected the fact that these commodities were produced at a relatively low cost because the workers in these industries were appallingly exploited.

With the exception of Leith, the Forth ports were small self-governing burghs which were centres of production of coal, salt and fish, each owning a small number of ships. Leith, as the port of Edinburgh with its large mercantile and banking interests, occupied a different position from the small ports and, as the records show, augmented its own ships by chartering those from nearby ports such as Prestonpans. While Edinburgh was a large centre, it owned only a quarter of the ships engaged in overseas trading and its importance lay in the enterprise of its mercantile class. The remaining burghs, while self-governing entities, were dependent upon the capital provided by various landowners who, owning mines and salt pans, built harbours in order to export their goods. These landowners, who included the Earls of Wemyss and Winton, may have owned ships outright but they also took shares in ships, together with merchants in neighbouring small burghs. This enabled the merchants to obtain resources for further developments to trade on their own account.

The 15 seaports of the outer Forth, ranging in size from those owning only one ship, such as Elie, to Kirkcaldy, a busy port owning 16 ships, made up an enterprising group of trading centres. Although independent to a large extent, as seafaring communities they were all well aware of home and overseas market developments in the eastern seaboard of Scotland as well as in England and in Holland. Many of the masters of ships carrying cargoes into Leith would have taken the opportunity to ascertain the prospect of future cargoes with the merchants of that port because of their extensive trading relationships. While Leith may not have owned as many ships as, say, Kirkcaldy, it was Scotland's major port chartering local and foreign ships for its export and import trade and would have provided trading opportunities for shipowners in other Forth Ports.

Ports and cargoes

The ports from which the *George* sailed with cargoes of salt and coal were Port Seton, Cockenzie and Elphinstoune in the Lothians, and Wemyss and Methil in Fife. These were, at that time, no more than small havens with limited pier facilities capable of loading and unloading ships up to 30 or 40 tons. Larger ships would lie offshore in sheltered waters and load or discharge their cargoes into lighters or keills. If the haven had a good sandy bottom, cargoes would be taken out to the ship by horse and cart when the tide was out.

Cockenzie was a small haven in use as early as the fifteenth century. The local landowner, the Earl of Winton, built a harbour there in 1630 so that the produce of his salt pans and mines could be exported. This port fell into disuse and was replaced by nearby Port Seton, built by the same Earl in 1635. Elphinstoune was a haven situated in Stirlingshire which has now disappeared. In his report of 1656 on the state of the revenue of Excise and Customs in Scotland, Thomas Tucker listed Elphinstoune as a port, stating that 'the Dutch mostly and some others chose to lade there because of the goodness of the coal and its measure'. Wemyss and Methil are recorded as ports in the *Old Statistical Accounts* for Fife and both were developed by the Earl of Wemyss for the purpose of exporting coal from his mines. Little trace now exists of the harbour at Wemyss. The harbour at Methil would appear to have been quite large for there is a record of a fee being paid by James Forrester for the service of a pilot so that the ship could enter and leave the port. The development of the mines at Methil led to its development into one of the largest coal-exporting ports on the east coast of Scotland (A. Graham p. 201–28).

The charts prepared by John Adair during the period 1680 to 1690 and published in 1703 were accompanied by a detailed description of the entrance to various ports and an excerpt dealing with the ports of 'Port Seaton', 'Cockeny', 'Prestounpans' and Newhaven is given below. This information on the position of rocks, depth of water and safe anchorages would have been essential for all shipmasters who intended using these ports and there would have been considerable demand for Adair's charts from English and Continental shipmasters. An extract from Adair's sailing directions is given on page 63.

It is doubtful whether local shipmasters would have purchased the charts as they would have acquired this information from long experience in using the ports.

Port-Seaton, is a good Tide Haven, beng covered from the N. and N.E. winds, by a hudge Peir of stone, that's Built out with a large bosome from the East corner of a clean little Bay; the Entry is clear, but not very broad, for there are ledges of Rocks that run a good peice off from the south side, and have readily a Beacon on the Point of them, so that coming in, you must keep closs along the head, and then bear up, and make fast to the Key. Here at a stream Tide, there are 15, 16. Foot water, and 10. in a neep, and it's full Sea on the Change Day about two of the Cloak.

At the back of the Peir there are riffs of Rocks stretching a good way out from the Land, and there are others that run off from them, a great way East along the shoar, about half a Mile from it, without which it's clean sand and 2. Fathiom Water closs, a litle farther 3. come no nearer, for they are covered by half Tide, and Ships borrowing upon the shoar have Wracked on them. The ordinary Road is about a Mile right of the Harbour, in 4, or 5. Fathom, but there is good clean ground on all hands.

This is one of the chiefest Ports, in all the Frith for Coal and Salt; for Ships of great burdeen may Load here in a Tide or two.

From Port-Seaton to Leith it's near 3. Leagues West over a long and hollow Bay; the thoar all the way is low, and for the most part sandy, and in some places Ebbs dry very far out, so that the Harbours that are there are none of the best.

A litle peice, West from Port-Seaton is Cockeny, where are some very good Houses, and a great many Salt-Pans; here also there is a Harbour within a stone Peir, but the Entry being very narrow its not much frequented now: The shoar on both sides of this is Rocky, and a litle off there is a Rock that appears not till low Water.

At the West end of Cockeny, there is a long riff called the Silly Craig, that runs a good way out from the Land, and within that the shoar turns in, and makes a Bay towards Prestounpans; a Town above a Mile in length, Built closs along a very foul Coast. Here are many good Houses, and a number of Salt-Pans, and albeit there is no Port, yet its a place of very good Trade: About half a Mile right off from this, are the Heccles a long tract of Rocks, stretching along the shoar W. S. W. from the Silly Craig, and not seen but at low Water and stream Tide; half a Mile without there is good Anchor Ground in 4, or 5. Fathom, and its alsso clean within them, where sometimes in Summer Ships ly to Unload.

The only effective means of transporting coal was by sea as it was difficult to transfer by land due to the lack of good roads. Some English mine owners built special roadways for small carts to convey the coal from the mine to the harbour. In Scotland, the Earl of Wemyss is reported to have built a wagonway to Methil, some two miles long, at the end of the eighteenth century, and early in the same century a track was built from Tranent coalfields to the harbour at Cockenzie. With the availability of cheap labour and the small size of cargoes, it is likely that the coal carried by the *George* reached harbour on the backs of men or pack horses. Where flat sandy beaches were not available owners of mines built quays on sheltered parts of the coast to provide a small haven for ships. With the development of markets and the increased size of ships, better facilities were required and if the landowners, who were usually the owners of the mines, had capital, the existing quays were extended, thus increasing the capacity of the harbours. The expenditure on these quays was very much to the benefit of the mine owner for without these limited means of loading ships it would not have been possible for coal and other products of the area to reach their markets.

The coal producers of Lothian and Fife were in a more advantageous position than many of their counterparts in England whose mines were, in many cases, not close to the coast or a navigable river. The Tyne coalfields, being close to the sea and a navigable river, were the main supplier of coal to English towns, especially London, and were the principal competitors of the Scots. The volume of the trade developed by the Tyne required a large number of ships to carry the product, many of which were locally owned and carried no other cargo than coal (Duckham Vol I, p. 209–17). Because these ships specialised in the transport of coal their freight rates were low and this enabled them to obtain markets both in England and the Continent to the exclusion of the smaller number of Scots ships.

While the Forth was a large producer of coal, its output was only a quarter of that of the Tyne in 1690. Some of the Scottish coal was cheaper and was of excellent quality in comparison with English coal and these factors, as the record of exports shows, enabled Scottish coal to find a market in England (Hatcher p. 62). The Scots had one large market for their coal in the seventeenth century and that was Rotterdam, as some Scots coal particularly suited the requirements of the brewery industry of that city because it burned more quickly than English coal (Smout p. 189).

Salt had been produced in the Firth of Forth since medieval times because of the availability of coal essential to its production, and there was a large export trade with England and the Scandinavian countries. This trade enabled Scotland to have the currency to pay for imports of timber from Norway and the Baltic states and merchandise from England. By the 1680s this trade had declined because of the availability of bay salt from France, Portugal and Spain. The English market was also supplied by the salt masters of the Tyne, who also had plenty of cheap coal available to heat the salt pans.

Bay salt was superior to Scots sea salt because it contained far fewer impurities, thus making the preserved product, be it meat or fish, more pleasant to eat. Part of the problem with Scots salt was that the main concern of the owners of the pans in the eighteenth century was high production without much consideration being given to the elimination of impurities. The Dutch took six times as long to make salt because of the time taken to draw off impurities, a process which increased the cost but ensured a market because of its quality. Continental bay salt had one disadvantage, which was its price, and, due to the high cost of transport, this factor ensured that the Scots could sell a large proportion of their product in the domestic market. Locally-produced salt was used in preserving food supplied to ships because owners wished to keep costs low and were not too concerned with the quality of food provided on their ships (Whatley p. 5–6).

Some salt producers, however, did make efforts to improve the quality of their product and this fact, together with the low cost of production and transport, enabled cargoes of salt to be taken to Norway and London in 1687 and 1688. Both the Scottish and the English salt industries enjoyed a period of prosperity after the declaration of war with France in 1689 which cut off continental supplies. It is a matter of regret that, because the outport records for Leith and Prestonpans do not exist after 1691, the extent of trade with England and Scandinavia in salt cannot be ascertained for the 1690s.

Salt was not an easy commodity to transport because it absorbed moisture and tended to shift when in bulk. Because of these factors, salt was sometimes packed in sacks, which had the disadvantage of taking up more space and reducing the tonnage carried. The *George*'s accounts record the purchase of sacking to make a tarpaulin to cover the hatches when the ship was carrying salt to avoid the cargo getting wet. It would have been difficult to avoid water reaching the cargo because the deck would have been awash during bad weather and, despite the efforts of the crew to seal the joints, the salt would have absorbed a good deal of moisture making it difficult to unload.

Exports

Exports from the ports of Prestonpans, Port Seton, Fisherrow and Dunbar are recorded in the customs outport record for the Precinct of Prestonpans for the period from November 1681 to November 1691 (NAS E72/21-15 16 21 22). The records for the early part of the period do not always cover a full year and contain very few entries of imports and exports. The records from November 1689 to November 1691 show that there was a considerable increase in the number of ships dealt with by the ports of the Precinct.

These customs records provide details of ships carrying dutiable cargoes and therefore took no account of ships engaged on the coasting trade. In addition to the movement of ships engaged in conventional trading, there were quite a few ships which would at one time or another have been engaged in smuggling goods into the country. The only means of ascertaining the movement of ships to and from a port would be by analysis of harbour records which would have recorded payment for anchorage by all ships, regardless of the cargo carried, and the only harbour records which exist for the seventeenth century are for the port of Aberdeen. The period 1687 to 1691 includes customs records covering two complete years, 1688–89 and 1690–91, the records for the intervening years being lost or incomplete. An analysis of the number of ships, their cargoes and destination for these two years is provided in Table 7.

This record of the movement of ships covers too short a period to enable any valid generalisation on the development of trade to be made. They do, however, reflect the situation shown by the statistics compiled by Professor Smout on the exports from the Precinct during the period 1680–86. These show that the majority of the ships from Prestonpans went to Holland and England, with Norway, France and the Baltic ports forming the next largest group (Smout Appendix I). Scotland imported a considerable amount of timber from Norway and wine from France, so it is not surprising that merchants endeavoured to obtain markets for salt in these and other countries to obtain the currency to pay for these imports. Scotland at that time was faced with increasing competition from England in her traditional overseas markets and would have been forced to seek markets elsewhere in order to obtain foreign currency.

The number of ships exporting goods from the Precinct of Prestonpans for 1688–89, 1690–91 and those of the port of Leith for 1692 are given below and from these figures it would appear that Leith was not as active as the ports comprising the Precinct. The figures of exports from Leith are taken from a survey carried out by the Convention of Royal Burghs in 1692.

Precinct of Prestonpans		Leith
1688–89	1690–91	1692
32	61	23

However, this comparison is misleading as the survey only recorded voyages made by the 13 ships which were owned by Leith or Edinburgh merchants. Leith at that time was Scotland's major port and carried out a considerable trade with other countries, with many cargoes being carried by English and foreign-owned ships. The charges for Leith were high because it was a large, port, and local merchants would have used small neighbouring ports such as Prestonpans and Port Seton because their charges were lower and their cargoes would have been loaded and unloaded in less time. This use of these small ports by ships which were chartered by Leith merchants greatly increased the number of ships employed and makes any comparison with Leith's exports unrealistic. These ports were burghs of barony and were owned or controlled by major local landowners such as the Earl of Winton and had by 1672 the same privileges as royal burghs, such as the right to engage in foreign trade and fix charges for use of their ports.

Table 7   Exports from Precinct of Prestonpans, 1688/89 and 1690/91.
(Source NAS E72/21, 1516 21 22)

1688/89			1690/91		
Cargoes	*No. of Ships*		*Cargoes*	*No. of Ships*	
Coal	7		Coal	12	
Salt	21		Salt	28	
Skins			Skins	15	
Tallow			Tallow	3	
Wool	4		Wool	3	
		32			61
Destination			*Destination*		
Coal	London	2	Coal	London	2
	Holland	4		Holland 2	10
		6			12
Salt	England	18	Salt	England	1
	France	2		France	2
	Holland	2		Danzig	1
		22		Holland	10
				London	4
Other	Holland	2		Norway	4
	London	2		Denmark	3
		4		Sweden	3
		32			28
			Skins	Holland	12
				Flanders	2
				Danzig	1
					15
			Tallow	London	3
					3
			Wool	London	1
				Holland	2
					3
					61

Scotland had a valuable formal trading link or staple, based at Veere, in Holland, which originated in the sixteenth century. The agreement was that only the following goods were allowed to enter the country without paying duty: skins, hides, woollen textiles, salmon, tallow and beef. The town officials of Veere ensured that harbour charges were kept at reasonable levels and, more importantly, that cargoes were unloaded and stored without delay. Veere's importance as a trading port was in decline by the 1680s because of the growth of the port of Rotterdam, which had become a major European trading centre with a large import and export trade. The port had the advantage of good facilities for unloading and storing cargoes and merchants willing to purchase and store goods because they had extensive trading contacts throughout Europe. It had, in addition, a large number of Scots merchants living there who acted as agents for both fellow countrymen and Dutch merchants.

During the 1680s Scotland's trade with Europe declined because of the high import duties imposed by Holland and France. The duty on Scots coal was three times that imposed on English coal. A similar situation arose with salt. The Scots seemed to have been particularly discriminated against with regard to duty on this product. According to a statement made to the Privy Council Scotland, salt 'pays 18/8 per weigh where French and Spanish salt pays no mor as a shilling' (Smout p. 230). The export of this commodity to London in 1688 is of significance. Labourers in the Scottish salt pans during this period were poorly paid, and costs of production were very low reflecting the cheapness of coal, and it may have been possible for salt to be sold in London at a competitive rate despite the high duty. England, a large importer of goods, had its own internal supplies of coal and salt, and imports from Scotland would only have been made if prices were lower than those charged by their English counterparts. The fact that the East Lothian ports could find a market for coal and salt was proof that their costs were low.

Imports

An analysis of imports of goods into the Precinct of Prestonpans during the years 1688–89 and 1690–91 confirms that the countries which traditionally had exported goods to Scotland remained unchanged. The following table records the number of ships bringing cargoes into the Precinct.

The source of Table 8 is custom records for the precinct and may not reflect the true total of ships bringing goods into the country. Because of the inadequacy of the customs services at that time numerous ships landed cargoes in quiet stretches of the coast to avoid paying duty. It was also a common practice for ships to land part of their cargo in some small port and then sail to their destination where the remainder would be declared. The cargoes from Norway and Denmark were timbers of various types and sizes which were used for house- and shipbuilding. Northern Scotland had pine forests but did not have the industrial skills to fell, cut and transport the timber to the domestic markets and was forced to import timber from countries with a well-established wood producing industry. Scotland had well-developed trading levels with Sweden, who supplied the country with all its requirements for iron over a long period. The demand for wine from Spain was limited to the nobility and the well-to-do merchant class, with other Scots at that time making

Table 8 *Number of ships bringing cargoes into the Precinct of Prestonpans from European countries.* (Source NAS E 72/21 15 21 22)

	1688–89	1690–91
Holland	60	28
Norway	12	20
England/London	3	12
Sweden	1	4
Hamburg	2	—
Denmark	—	2
Spain	—	1
Greenland	—	1
Unidentified	—	5
	78	**73**

do with beer, a very much cheaper drink. It was Holland and to a lesser extent England that sent Scotland the greatest variety of goods including textiles, drugs for the apothecary, dye such as madder, window glass, writing paper, spices, lemons, seeds, fruit trees, flax and iron. The need to import goods is an illustration of the lack of industry and skilled men in the country during the seventeenth century, a position which continued until the middle of the next century.

A copy of an extract from the Kirkcaldy customs outport register dated 9 July 1690 is given in Figure 21 and a transcript of this document is given below. This lists the goods imported by ten merchants together with the marks which would have been used to identify their individual bundles or boxes (E 72/9/28).

July 9   Reported the John and David of Kirkcaldy David Williamson and Mr James Davidson Merchants they declared upon their soloem oath that bulk has not been broken of their said ship of any Merchants good since they came from their loading port directly or indirectly neither of them nor any of their company this they declare to be atrueth to the both of their knowledge and they shall answer to God having only aboard.

One bagg cont. <u>gaulls</u>	*Thirty four thousand barrell hoops*
One bagg cont. gaulls	*seven casks jumps 2= Barrells ditto*
One Box cont. indigo	*five Boxes Indigo*
One Bundle cont. turkey skins	*One <u>runlett</u> of <u>Aronatta</u>*
One Bundle cont. writing paper	*One Barrell of fastick wood*
Eighteen Barrells cont. Jumps	*One cask logwood*
One Barrell cont. gingerbread	*One bundle cont. <u>wrott brase</u>*
Four <u>hhds</u> vinegar	*One basket cont. glass bottles*

Two hhds vinegar
One bundle cont. bend leather
Four barrells cont. lead sheath
One small parcell cont. *thion* silke
One hhd cont. Jumps
Twenty Barrells lead sheath
Eight Barrells lead
Two Baggs of new wool *Cairds*
Two hhds Jumps
Three hhds jumps
One hhd Jumps
One Box cont. wrott pewter

One box cont. Indigo
One hhd cont. *copperas*
One bundle cont. *pressing papers*
One bundle cont. pressing papers
Seven hundred pound unmade Tin
One Bar of lead

Gaulls:	Contemporary word for oak gall which was used to make ink.
Jumps/Jump:	Strips of leather used to build up the heel of a shoe.
Hhds:	Hogs heads equivalent to a quarter of a ton.
Thion:	Unknown substance.
Cairds:	Cards, for carding wool.
Wrott:	Wrought or decorated.
Runlett:	Small barrel containing three to four gallons.
Aronatta:	This is possibly sweet-smelling spices.
Brase:	Brass.
Copperas:	Sulphate of iron used in dyeing cloth black or making ink.
Pressing Paper:	It is not possible to ascertain the use of this type of paper.

Cargoes carried by the *George*

The disbursement records give only brief details of cargo taken to Scotland by the *George* and it is fortunate that the customs outport records provide information on these cargoes. On entering a port a master had to report to the customs giving details of his cargo, including the name of all merchants and the identifying marks made on their goods, and to produce all documents relating to the cargo such as bills of lading, cockets and transfers. In addition 'he shall answer to all such other questions concerning the direct quantity of goods laden in the said ship as shall be demanded of him by the Collector'. The collector would then appoint a waiter who would check that the goods and merchandise therein was laden, cleared and discharged.

The last entry in the accounts for the voyage to Norway reads: '3 days for a man to help unload the ship 18s 0d'. This is odd for there is no entry in the custom register of a cargo landed by the *George* or any record of freight charges. Cockenzie, where the ship unloaded the goods, was a small port and customs officials may not always have been in attendance, thus enabling the cargo to be unloaded duty-free.

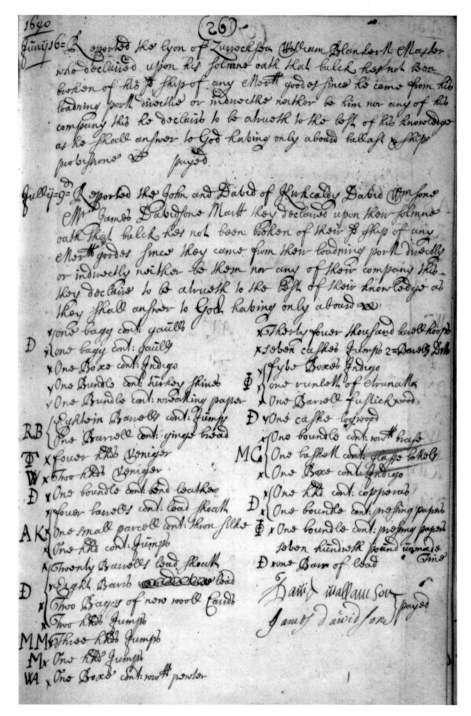

Figure 21   Extract from the customs outport register of Kirkcaldy, 9th July 1690 E72/9/28. Reproduced by kind permission of the Keeper of the Records of Scotland.

The information on the cargoes imported and exported, the name of the ship and her master were then recorded in considerable detail in the Precinct's outport books. Two extracts from the Prestonpan outport book for 1688–89 giving details of the cargo carried on the ship's sixth voyage from Rotterdam in 1689 are given below (NAS E 72/21/16). As he was required by the custom regulations, James Forrester had to depond or swear on oath that 'he hath not brocken bulk in the scottis seas' and that details recorded about his cargo were correct.

Reported the George of Port Seaton from Rotterdam James Forrester master who depond that he hath not brocken bulk in the scottis seas his p[rese]nt voyage and that his Loadening Consists of on hodgshead and ane matt marked I[]II. Four hodgsheads and ane matt marked WG Ane matt marked IG: Nyn barrells marked MT. Fyve matts three hodgsheads ane Caske marked [] Fyve barrells and ane hodgheads marked MC tuo hodgheads on firkin marked [] ane small matt marked AB six ould Chairs and three matts marked IF ane old press and tuo old tables marked idem on small matt marked M ane quantitie of onions and this is all and is truth as he shall ansser to god.

Jas. Forrester

Reported the George of Port Seatoune James Forrester master from Rotterdame who depones that he hathe not broken bulk directlie nor indirectlie since he cam withing the scottis seas and that his loadning consists of the par[tic]lure followeing merks and is underwritten viz fortie sex barrells great and small ane halfe bale of mader eightine matts and pocks ane hundered and nyntie sex boxes of lamb bleake ten coyles of wheal ropes ane litle box telve runile of gray peper tuo hundered and fyve gades of irone ane hundered and nynteine irone pots and ketles sextie thrie pound of weights for weighting ane cradle all marked WC: Ane old press ane old table and ane furme and two baskets with lame waire[1] ane old glass caise two irone ketles and iron port two muskets for the shipes use all marked IF: Tuo mats marked [] two small baskets of lame waire two old boords and ane small press ane cradle ane barrell of flinstones and this is the truthe as he shall answear to God.

Jas. Forrester

The initials IF should read JF for James Forrester as, included in goods carried with this mark, are two muskets for the ship's use and the purchase of these muskets is recorded in the accounts. The term 'matt' refers to a measure for flax but this is the only recognisable measure on the list; the terms 'lamp', 'bleak', 'wheal', 'ropes', 'gades of iron' are terms which have fallen into disuse. It was the custom to allow members of the crew of a ship to carry a small amount of cargo free of charge if space allowed and many seamen took advantage of this in order to do trading on their own account.

Apart from the furniture, the other items had recognised commercial use. Madder was a blue dye used in linen making, a growing industry in Scotland at that time. The hogsheads and barrels would have been used for keeping wine and fish. The iron would have been used by the local blacksmiths. The other items of the cargo such as six old chairs, an old press and tables, an old glass case, and two old boards are also of significance. Scotland at that time was a poor country in comparison with England and Holland and few people would have been able to purchase such goods from a native craftsman. Such skilled men would have resided in the large burghs, with only a small number of the population having the resources to pay for their services. Holland, however, was at that time a rich country with a considerable trade with Europe and abroad and many of its citizens enjoyed a high standard of living. They would be able to replace furniture as it became old knowing that the originals would find a ready market with seamen from poorer countries. Rotterdam being a prosperous city had many craftsmen working within its boundaries and they would have supplied iron kettles and pots and the lame ware of earthenware or china.

Ships owned by Forth ports 1688–1692

There were not many ships owned by the ports in the area between Dunbar, Leith and Kirkcaldy in the period 1687–90 when the *George* was trading which were capable of undertaking voyages between these ports, the Continent and London. The information on the ships owned by individual ports during this period comes from two sources. The first is the port books maintained by customs which recorded movements of various vessels carrying dutiable goods. The second is a survey made by the Convention of Royal Burghs in 1690 into the state and condition of every burgh in Scotland and which was completed by July 1692 (J.D. Marwick p. 566–660) This source gave the number of ships owned by individual burghs together with their tonnage. The survey was carried out to ascertain the resources available to burghs in order that they could be assessed for their potential to develop trade. Not all the burghs replied to the request for information, and many small burghs indicated that they owned ships without providing information on their tonnage. These were not large ports so it can be assumed that the vessels themselves were small and not capable of undertaking a deep sea voyage. A copy of the Accompt (account) of the Ships of Leith prepared for the Convention by the Shor (shore) Maister is given in Figure 22.

Information concerning the ships owned by individual ports was obtained from David Dobson's booklets *The Mariners of the Lothians 1600–1700* and *The Mariners of Kirkcaldy & West Fife 1600–1700* (which list voyages undertaken by individual ships) and from custom records for the Precincts of Prestonpans and Kirkcaldy (NAS E 72/21-15 16 21 22; NAS E 72/9 24 27). Using these sources a list of vessels was compiled which were described as being 'of a port' and it is noticeable that a few vessels with the same name appeared in the lists for individual ports. A list of the dates of the voyages undertaken by these apparent duplications showed

56	STATE AND CONDITION OF THE BURGHS OF SCOTLAND.					
REPORTS, 1692.		Accompt of the Ships of Leith the 17th May 1692.				
EDINBURGH.	SKIPPERS OF SHIPS.	BURDEN. TUNS.	VALUE.	SKIPPERS OF BARKS.	BURDEN. TUNS.	VALUE.
	Captain James Kendall	90	8000	John Haigs	40	2000
	Captain James Simson	120	5000	John Achinmutie	36	1500
	Alexander Tait	150	8000	David Riehaye	25	900
	Robert Gray	100	6000	Charles Ranie, ane wark		
	Thomas Whyt	90	6000	Thomas Hendersone	25	900
	Thomas Riddell	100	3500	John Gair	16	500
	Thomas Weir	90	3000	John Kay	12	300
	Androw Simsone	70	3000	John Sime	30	1000
	Alexander Stivenson	130	5000	Gilbert Dick	20	600
	James Sutherland	90	6000	Walter Graige	15	500
	John Tait	60	4000	Mathew Barton	24	900
	James Law	90	6000	William Browne	24	900
	John Browne	140	8000	Malcolm Maccalla	30	1200
	SKIPPERS OF BARKS.			Alexander Gerve	16	700
	John Barr	40	1000	Walter Lesly	14	500
	John Mill	15	300			

This is the trew list given in by me. *Sic subscribitur :* Walter Learmont, shor maister.

Figure 22   Accompt of the ships of Leith, May 1692. Reproduced with permission from Aberdeen University Library.

that there was more than one vessel of the same name correctly described as being 'of a port' and some vessels described as being, for example, 'of Leith' on one voyage and on a later date being of another port with, however, the same master. By listing the voyages taken by vessels with the same name it was possible to determine whether they were the same vessel but ascribed to different ports or two ships with the same name. With the greater majority of the ships there was no difficulty in ascertaining that they were of a stated port. There were other ships where there was insufficient evidence to prove if there was duplication and only one vessel has been recorded as belonging to a particular port.

The port records for Leith, Kirkcaldy and Prestonpans do not exist for 1691 so it is not possible to make a direct comparison with the number of vessels recorded as belonging to individual ports in the survey (on the assumption that much of the survey was carried out between 1690 and 1691). From Dobson, 16 ships and their masters were identified as belonging to Leith in 1691–92, three more than the list number provided to the convention. A similar situation arose with Kirkcaldy where the number of vessels engaged in trading with Europe was 20, six more than the number given in the survey. Table 11 shows the number of ships trading from the Precinct of Kirkcaldy in 1688–89 and 1690–91 as 18 and 19 respectively which is confirmation that the figure of 20 in Table 9 for the port is a reasonable estimate.

The number of vessels trading from Prestonpans and Port Seton given in Table 9 is seven which is well below the total for 1690–91 of 15 which is given in Table 11. A similar position arises with the number of ships trading from Prestonpans and Port Seton where the total supplied to the convention for these ports, which is given in Table 9, is seven and the number taken from customs records is 15. It is very likely that some ships owned by the ports were lost during the period; however such losses would not account for the difference between the two records. The figures given in the survey must, however, be taken as underestimating the total number of ships trading from Forth ports during this period.

A summary of the number of ships belonging to Forth ports is given in Table 9 and is based on the survey, customs records and Dobson. The total number of ships is 74 and, if ships with a tonnage of between 30 and 45 are excluded as being too small to undertake long voyages, this would reduce the number of ships capable of trading with England and the Continent to 68. Because of the likelihood that the survey understates the number of ships it would be reasonable to assume that

Table 9 Number of ships owned by Forth ports during 1688–1692.

			Tonnage			
Ports	unknown	30–45	50–80	85–95	100–150	Total
Leith	3		2	5	6	16
Kirkcaldy	6	3	5		6	20
Pittenweem			1		1	2
Elie			1			1
Dysart			1			1
Crail				1		1
Anster	2	1	1			4
Wemyss	2					2
Burntisland	3					3
Port Seton					1	1
Prestonpans	6					6
Fisherow	2					2
Bo'ness	4					4
Queensferry					7	7
Stirling		2				2
Dunbar	2					2
	30	6	11	6	21	74

the number of Scots ships trading from Forth Ports at the same time as the *George* would have been about 80 to 90.

Voyages made by the *George* and Firth of Forth ships

The trading carried out by the *George* was very similar to that carried out by ships of her size and which belonged to ports of the Firth, with the greater majority of cargoes being carried to Holland and England. The pattern of the ship's voyages set out in Table 10 shows that with the exception of the winters 1688–89 and 1689–90 the ship did not spend much time in port. In medieval times the Hanseatic ports forbade ships to carry out voyages during the winter months in order to reduce losses due to bad weather. By the end of the seventeenth century ships were under no such restrictions although very few ships undertook voyages during the months of December, January and February and the port records show only a small number of cargoes being landed during this period. These were, very likely, cargoes carried by ships which were delayed in returning to Scotland for various reasons.

The noticeable feature of Table 10 is the time taken to complete voyages, a factor which must have made the cost of operating a ship of this period relatively high. These seventeenth-century ships with their bluff bows and high superstructure were slow even with a good following wind. Since winds vary in speed and direction a ship would travel many more miles to reach its destination than a vessel powered by steam. Also, vessels entering busy ports such as Rotterdam and London would have to wait in the river before getting to a quay to unload. With limited space on the quays, a ship's stay in port could be a long one. Customs officials also took time to check cargoes and assess duty and it would have required a master with experience in dealing with customs and harbour officials to ensure that his ship and its cargo were dealt with without undue delay.

In order to make comparison with the voyage made by other Firth ships, the number of voyages undertaken by the *George* within the customs year (November to November) is given in Table 10, which shows that the number of voyages varied considerably.

The number of voyages undertaken to England and the continent by ships from the Precincts of Prestonpans (NAS E 72/21 15 16 21 22) and Kirkcaldy (E 72/9 24 27) have been analysed using the outport records for these Precincts, and the results are given in Table 11. The periods taken for Prestonpans and Kirkcaldy differ slightly and this is because an analysis was only made of outport records which covered a complete year. It was noticeable that only a small number of ships made two or three voyages each year and these would be undertaken within the period March to December and made by experienced shipmasters. The number of voyages undertaken by some ships varied, with some making three voyages one year and only one the next. However, the majority of ships making two voyages in 1688–89 made the same number of voyages in the following year. The majority of ships however undertook only one voyage during the summer months when there was

Table 10 Voyages made by the George.

Period of voyage	Port	Customs year	No. of voyages	Length of voyage (days)	Time in home port
* Mar 87 – last May 1687	Not known	1686–87	1	75	
1 Jul 87– Mar 1688	Norway	1687–88		260	45
2 May 88 – 1 Jul 1688	London	1687–88	3	45	45
3 Jul 88 – end Sep 1688	London	1687–88		75	15
4 Oct 88 – last Dec 1688	Rotterdam	1688–89		75	15
5 1 Apr 89 – last Jun 1689	Rotterdam	1688–89	3	90	90
6 Mid Jul 89 – last Sep 1689	Campvere	1688–89		75	15
7 1 Nov 89 – mid Apr 1690	London	1689–90	1	165	30
8 last Jul 90 – 9 Dec 1690	London	1690–91	1		75

* There is very little information in the accounts about this voyage.

Table 11 Number of voyages made by ships owned by ports in the Precincts of Prestonpans and Kirkcaldy.

PRESTONPANS*				KIRKCALDY			
1688–89		1690–91		1688–89		1690–91	
Ships	Voyages	Ships	Voyages	Ships	Voyages	Ships	Voyages
3	9	1	3	2	6	4	12
3	6	3	6	9	18	4	8
14	14	11	11	7	7	11	11
20	29	15	20	18	31	19	31

* Including voyages of the *George*

little risk of bad weather. As the customs records only show vessels which had cargoes which were dutiable, it is not possible to ascertain whether the ships which made only one voyage to England or the Continent were also engaged in carrying fish, which was not liable for duty, or were carrying goods to another part of Scotland.

The shor maister provided in addition to the number of ships of Leith, details of the voyages undertaken by some of these ships during a 12-moth period in either 1690 or 1691. Also Leith was at this time the largest port on the east coast of Scotland. It is noticeable that only one ship made more than two voyages during the period. A copy of this statement is given below. The *George* was therefore one of a very small group of ships making two or three voyages a year to the Continent and England from the Precincts of Kirkcaldy and Prestonpans. This level of activity shows that the owners were able to obtain markets for coal and salt in the face of what must have been considerable competition from English coal and salt producers. This success must, however, be contrasted with an inability to obtain cargoes on the return voyage, thus leading to the *George* operating at a loss over the eight voyages.

Accompt of Shiping belonging to the merchants of Edinburgh for twelve moneths by past.

Kendalls ship twice to Holland, with lead ure and sheep skins.

Simpsons, trade twice to Holland with coalls and wooll.

Alexander Tait, twice to Holland with coalls, at present ane transact ship in France with Canon and Buchan.

Robert Gray, twice to Holland with coalls, sheep skins, and wooll.

Thomas Whyt, twice to Holland with coalls, sheep skins, and wooll.

Thomas Riddell, once to Hamburgh with returns of mumbear, some quantity of brandie, and once to France with return of wyne.

Thomas Weir, twice to London with coalls and some packs of linnen cloath, quherof the most pairt belonged to Glasgow.

Andrew Simpson to London, with coalls and some packs of linnen cloath, whereof the most pairt belonged to strangers, with some packs of drest leather belonging to merchants heir.

George Wood, twice to Holland with coalls and sheep skins.

Alexander Stevinsone, twice to Amsterdam with coalls.

James Sutherland, once to Hamburgh with returns of mumbear and some brandie, and now at Spain.

John Tait, imployed by the publict at Innerlochie.

James Law, once at London with shouldiers, being balanced with coalls.

John Brown, once to Bilbo and not yeit reteired.

Item, thrie Swades or Damask ships, in all thrie hunder tunns, with wynes from France.

Item, three ships belonging to the merchants all lost comeing from France with wynes.

Item, as to the consumption of malt, the same is computed to be about 500 bolls per week.

Item, to the trade with the barks the same is all inland trade with corns and coalls, except two barks who are at present in the Sound with herrings on the merchants accompt.

Chapter Four

Contracts and instructions to shipmasters

As early as the sixteenth century it was standard practice for shipowners to have two written contracts with merchants wishing to have goods delivered. The first was a charter party and the other a bill of lading. These examples of contracts set out in simple terms the conditions for the carriage of goods. When disputes arose between ship owners and owners of cargoes, cases based upon the conditions in these documents were brought to the Admiralty Courts. As a result, considerable changes were made to the wording in later Charter Partys and Bills of Lading.

Charter party

A charter party was a formal agreement between a merchant wishing to consign designated goods to a stated port or ports and the master and owner of a stated vessel. This agreement was called a charter party from the French *charter partie* which was a contract setting out the terms for the collection and delivery of the goods in a stated ship. An example of a charter party is given below.

Charter Party dated 1707 for Voyage from Speymouth to Leith

At Portsoy July the second seventeen hundred and seven years. It is condescended and finally agreed upon between the parties following viz: Wm Gregorie in ferrie parton Craig Master of the Janet of Dundee upon the on part, and James Innes Junior, Mert in Elgin on the other part in manner following. That is to say the sd Wm Gregorie fraughts his sd ship now lying inn the harbour of portsoy takeing in a loadening of the Chancellours victual; and how soon it pleases God they liver the same at Leith. The sd Wm obliedges himselfe to sail with his sd ship to Spey mouth with all convenient diligence wind and weather serveing, and ther to have his ship wind and water tight under and above with a sufficient Crew of mariners and to ly eight work weather ly dayes for takeing in an loadening of victual from the sd James or any in his name haveing his power: and from thence to sail to the south firth, and at Leith waite orders to any other port his sd Mert shall happen to sell in south firth: and in the mean time obliedges him selfe that none of the victuall shall be wronged any manner of way by him or his Crew, and at the livering port appointable by the sd Mert he is to ly other eight work weather ly dayes for unloadeing the sd victual, which the sd skipper obliedges him to deliver in good order and condition, (heating and danger of provateers only excepted) For the which cause the sd James Innes obliedges him to pay tem pund scots in name of fraught for ilk chalder of bear and double chalder of meal livered out at livering port, and that within fourtie eight houres after unloading as also an boll meal and barrell of ale in name of Caplaken with avarag confirm to sea custom. And both parties obliedges them selves to the performace of the premisses each to other under the failzie of fourtie pund scots of liquidat expenses payable by the partie broaker to the partie performer and willing to perform by and attour performance Consenting to the reg[ist]ra[tio]n hereof in any Judges Books competent that all execu[tio]n needfull may pass theron in form as effers And to that effect Constitutes Their pro[]res etc In witness whereof thir pr[esen]ts (written by Mr Charles Anderson in portsoy) are sub[scribi]t with bothe the sd parties hands place and time forsd befor witnesses Wm Key Schoul Mr at portsoy and the sd Mr Charles writer hereof and Patrick Kirk seaman aboard the sd ship.

William Gregorie
James Innes

This document follows a standard pattern giving the name of the ship, its master and owner and the name(s) of the merchant whose goods are to be carried, details of the cargo and the 'ly dayes' or time allowed for loading and unloading of the cargo, as the penalties for late delivery are explicitly stated. The term heating may refer to the danger of fire due to the nature of the cargo.

Bill of lading

Before the master of a sixteenth-century ship could leave port with a cargo, he would have had to sign a bill of lading which stated that the goods specified as cargo had been put on board his ship and that these goods would be delivered in good order to a stated port. The bill, which was prepared in triplicate, was a receipt for the cargo and acted as a memorandum between the owner of the ship and the shipper of the goods. The master would retain one copy as proof of the goods carried on the ship when he was boarded by harbour and customs officials at his destination. The description of cargoes in the bills was brief if the cargo consisted of one item such as coal or salt or timber. If, however, the cargo was mixed, details of the cargo would be listed on an attached sheet so that the master and the consignee(s) would be able to identify the separate parts of the cargo.

Two examples of bills of lading are shown in Figures 23 and 24 and as the writing is not very clear transcripts of these are given below. The first is a written document while the second is a printed form. In both cases, the conditions are clearly stated and the goods can be identified by descriptions or by consignor's marks. The *Happy James of Alloa* could well have brought a cargo of various goods from Rotterdam, for custom records for the Precinct of Inverness show that there were regular cargoes brought from that port which were unloaded in Spey or Findhorn, the two major ports in the Moray Firth at that time. The appearance of a large vessel in either of these ports would have been a much talked-about event and the master would have had little difficulty in arranging a return cargo with local merchants. The bill for the *John and Elizabeth* (Figure 24) has adequate space to detail the cargo of timber, iron and hemp and is on a form which was used through-out the eighteenth century and probably after that.

Bill of Lading of the Happy James of Alloa *(AC 9/381)*

Shipped by the grace of God in good order and well conditioned by his Grace George Duke of Gordon in and upon the good ship called the Happy James of Alloa whereof its Master under God for this present voyage John Morrison and now riding at anchor in Spey harbour and by God's grace bound for Leith in the South Firth. To say.

Two Venison pots covered, one four square box nailled up, one marable mortar with one timber pestle, one little metal mortar with one iron pestle, one waffle iron, one jack & wheel with its flight, one iron dripping pan with one standard, one brass pot with its cover, two spitts, one pair of iron raxes with two rings and 3 hinges upon one of them & two upon the other, a little spinning wheel, one barrell of salmon marked SD, one big trunk sealled, one white box sealled, one harn pock [poke] sealled all with one seall, as also two small boxes unsealled, with glasses in them both and are to be delivered in the like good order at the livering port (the danger of the seas only excepted) unto his Grace or his assigney he or they paying freight therefore in witness thereof the Master of the said ship hath subscribed these present at Spey Mouth the fifth day of October 1706.
            John Morrison

As lykewayes reseaved one little barrell and nine boxes which I oblige to deliver in lyke good order sea hazards excepted.
            John Morrison

As lykewayes one little bag, one little trunk, one box, one pair of jack boots, one crishie web, two fire shovels and two locks all which I oblige me to deliver in like good order at Leith sea hazard excepted.
            John Morrison

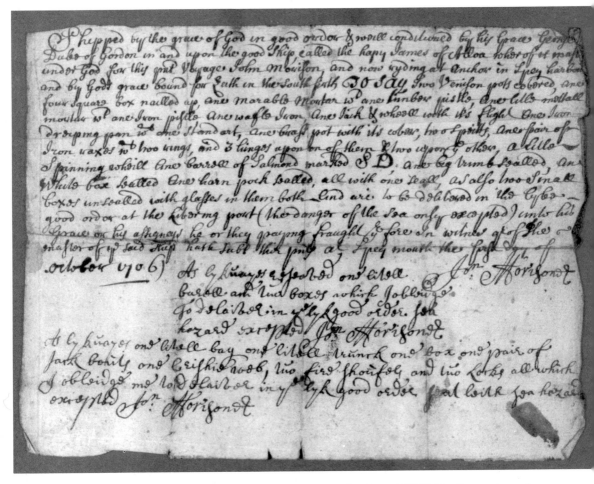

Figure 23   Bill of Lading of **Happy James of Alloa.** *AC9/381. Reproduced by kind permission of the Keeper of the Records of Scotland.*

The items listed in the bill were part of the household goods of the Duke of Gordon and show the range of equipment used in a nobleman's kitchen of that period.

Waffle iron: A contemporary piece of equipment which apparently has a long history.

Jack wheel   This was a type of spit which was attached to a fan arrangement
& flight: in the chimney which enabled the spit to turn in the updraught. Source: *Food in England* by Dorothy Hartley.

Harnt poke: Harnt was a shortened version of harden, a coarse linen or hemp. Source: *Concise Scottish Dictionary*.

Iron raxes: A set or bars to support a roasting spit. Source: *The Scots Thesaurus*.

As was the practice goods were marked by the individual shippers so that they could be identified when the ship reached its destination.

A case was submitted to the Admiralty Court involving the *Happy James of Alloa* because the ship was wrecked off Peterhead and the Duke of Gordon took action to recover part of the cargo which had been appropriated by some towns-people of that burgh.

> *Shipped by the Grace of God in good Order and well Conditioned, by Marjoribanks & Coutts in and upon the good Ship called the John & Elizabeth of Prestonpans whereof is Master under God for this present Voyage James Bell and now riding at Anchor in the Quays of Dantzig and by God's Grace bound for Anstruther to pay Thirty Four pieces black Oak Planks, Seventy Six bars Iron, Four Bundles Hemp and one equal fourth part of fifteen coyles white and tarred ropes for account of Mr James Graham being marked and numbred as in the Margent, and are to be delivered in the like good Order and well Conditioned at the aforesaid Port of Anstruther (the danger of the Seas only excepted) unto Mr James Graham or to his Assigns, he or they paying freight for the said Goods according to Charter Party with Primage and Avarage accustomed. In Witness whereof the Master or Purser of the said Ship hath affirmed to 3 Bills of Lading, all of this tenor and date, the one of which 3 Bills being accomplish'd, the other two to stand void. And so God send the good Ship to her desired Port in Safety. Amen. Dated in Dantzig November 1715*
>
> *James Bell*

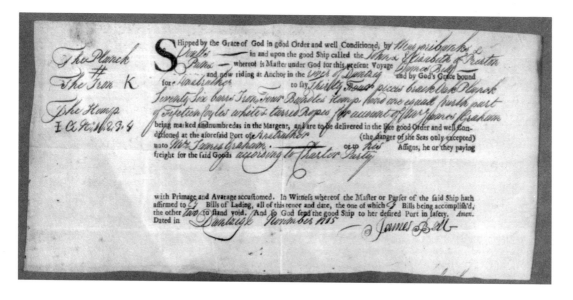

*Figure 24 Bill of Lading of the **John & Elizabeth** of Prestonpans (AC 9/ 467). Reproduced by kind permission of the Keeper of the Records of Scotland.*

These examples of a charter party and bills of lading contain terms which require explanation.

'Master unto God'. A shipmaster was described as such in Bills of Lading and the phrase describes the profession aptly. When a ship sailed from a port in the 17th century there was no means of communicating with the land and the Master was solely responsible for the safety of the ship, her crew and the cargo.

'The danger of the seas only excepted'. This term first appeared in about 1650 and gave rise to many cases appearing in the Admiralty Court when goods were not delivered in good order and the consignor claimed damages. These dangers were defined by the early courts as piracy, acts of God, the king's enemies and fire. Later bills defined these dangers in a specific manner to avoid any claim being the subject of a court case. The early bills were simple statements which were soon replaced as various court decisions required conditions and exceptions to be stated in a more explicit manner.

'Caplagen' is a term derived from the Dutch term *kaplaken* which became obsolete in the eighteenth century and was replaced by the term 'primage' without changing its meaning. Primage refers to the long-standing practice whereby the shipper of goods made a payment to the master and crew of the ship in order to ensure that care was taken of his goods when loading and unloading them and on their passage to their destination. 'Average' does not appear on the bill for the *Happy James* and may well have been a condition set out in the charter party and therefore not considered necessary to be repeated in the bill. The word 'accustomed' which sometimes followed the terms 'primage' and 'average' in these contracts implied that generally accepted practice in the transport of goods by sea would be followed. While 'average' could well cover a wide range of expenses, it was restricted to expenditure incurred by the ship on entering and leaving harbour. This would include light and anchorage dues, pilotage and berthage. An example of these charges paid on a voyage from Muldo to Leith in 1727 is given below (H. Marwick p. 56–57). Forrester did not detail how he arrived at the charges for average included in the disbursement record for various voyages although it is possible to arrive at a reasonably close figure to that given by him. The use of the term 'accustomed' implies that payment of primage and average would conform to customary practice.

In addition to the specific instructions contained in the charter party, the loading and delivering of a cargo to a designated port owner or merchants would also provide further instructions in a letter to the master. These would for example include a warning to check the quality of the cargo if the supplier was known for supplying inferior goods, or a request that he purchase certain goods if they were available at a reasonable price. Most owners would have had confidence in their masters to act in their interests, and the instructions would be brief and just give the names of agents in the port the cargo was being delivered to so that they could provide advice and information on a cargo for the return journey.

Evorage Bill On a Voage to Muldo from thence Leith for acownt of Jas. Traill and parteners

October ye 28th, 1727

To Pillotage from Muldo to Sea	16	6
To touage in and out of Frezerburgh	7	-
To Anchorage there	2	-
To a boatt Bringing us to ye Bay and helping to purchase our anchor	3	-
To two boats taking us in and outt from Stonehaven	11	-
Anchorage there	1	6
To anchorage and warping outt at Ely	3	6
At Leith - To Touage in	1	-
To Anchorage, Berth and Biconage	8	9
To Light of May	3	9
	£2 18	-

Edinburgh ye 26th January 1728

THO: JAMESON

This account is endorsed in James Traill's hand as follows:

$^2/_3$ to ye merchant	£1 18	8
$^1/_3$ to the ship	- 19	4
	£2 18	-

Chapter Five

Ransom and roup

James Forrester being input master of the Helen in a voyage from Eyemouth to Newcastle where he was to take in coals &c fro the defender's behoof and was to transport these with the other goods put aboard at Eyemouth to Hamburg and there to take in such goods as they should order and from thence to sail to Norway and there to take in timber and other goods to be put aboard there and to return to Eyemouth. When the ship had sailed but two leagues from Eyemouth in the voyage to Newcastle, the same was seized by a French privateer and thereafter ransomed for £180 sterling, for which the said James Forrester went hostage.' (AC 9/402)

The above description of the intended voyage of a ship and its seizure in April 1710 by a privateer is taken from the records of an Admiralty Court case which was held in Edinburgh between January and March 1711. The case in question was brought by Janet Johnston, wife of James Forrester, erstwhile master of the *George of Port Seton*, to make the owners of the *Helen* pay the ransom together with the expenses which were incurred by her husband in prison. She was a person of considerable character first to approach the owners of the ship for payment and, when being rebuffed by them, to engage the services of a lawyer so that she could enforce the rights of her husband by judicial process. As wife of a shipmaster Janet Johnston would have been aware that her husband had under Scots maritime law a right called lien which enabled him, subject to the approval of the court, to sell the *Helen* and have a preferential claim on the proceeds. The money so obtained would be used to pay any debts incurred by him by virtue of his position as shipmaster. She knew that unless she took action to obtain the monies due, her husband would stay in a French prison for a considerable period.

Before giving a description of the capture of the *Helen* and the subsequent court proceeding it is necessary to outline the prevailing situation for any shipmaster proposing to undertake a voyage from the Firth of Forth in 1710.

Since 1707 the French Navy had been employing a number of small well-armed ships to act as privateers to patrol the east coast of Britain with the objective of capturing ships. Their activities had the effect of severely limiting seaborne trade as shipowners were suffering losses in ships, cargoes and heavy penalties for the ransom of crew members. Trade was so badly affected that the Convention of Royal Burghs in 1708 made a plea to Queen Anne requesting the protection of the Navy for the reason that *'many of our ships have been taken of late by French Privateers who doe very much abound upon our coasts'* (J.D. Marwick p. 456).

In that year the Cruiser and Convoy Act was passed which authorised the use of naval ships to convoy merchant shipping. Action was taken by the Admiralty to put the convoy system into use in Scotland in 1709. The Government was forced to take this action for, in addition to the serious disruption to trade, the activities of the privateers in seizing cargoes was reducing the effectiveness of the naval blockade of French ports. While the Act allocated nine ships to the east coast of Scotland, only five ships carried out these convoy duties due to the demands made on the Royal Navy by the war (Mowat p. 280–81). The convoy system operated by these ships proved to be effective and the number of seizures made by privateers was considerably reduced. Nevertheless, the French still managed to disrupt trade during the periods when the convoys and their escorts had left the marshalling ports of Scapa Flow, Cromarty, Aberdeen and Leith because there were insufficient naval ships available to carry out regular convoy duties off the Scottish coast.

The introduction of the convoy system in 1710 was not the first time such a system had been operated on the east coast. During the Nine Years War which started in 1688, the English Government was concerned about the scale of operations carried out by groups of large privateers who were disrupting English and Scottish trade. Relationships between the Scots and the English were not good during the war due to the actions of the English Navy, and it was only the activities of privateers that made the Scots use a convoy system operated by the Royal Navy. In reality the Scots had no option but to join the convoy system, as prior to 1707 the country could only afford to provide three small armed ships to protect shipping in the Forth Estuary. These ships were no match for the well-armed privateers and it was only by 1696 that the Scots obtained three ships from London large enough to provide a defence against the French. The disbursement records of the *George* showed that on voyages in 1689 and 1690 payments were made so that the ship could join a convoy, and it is apparent that many Scottish ships used the system.

The East Lothian and Berwickshire coasts lay along the route taken by ships travelling between Scotland and England, within easy reach of privateers from French ports. When James Forrester was in Eyemouth he would have been informed of the danger of action by these privateers. In an attempt to avoid capture the *Helen* adopted the device of flying the flag of a neutral nation, and was named the *Hellena* of Stockholm. The privateer which would have been lying off the coast had a rig similar to other ships in the area and Forrester would not have considered the approaching vessel to be a threat until it was too late. The Master of the privateer would have assumed that the *Helen* was a British ship, boarded it and demanded to see the Bills of Lading and other documents. He then decided to obtain a ransom instead of capturing the ship and forced Forrester to sign a Form of Agreement on behalf of his owners to pay the sum of £180, presumably an estimate of the value of the ship and its cargo. It may seem remarkable that a shipmaster would surrender his vessel without a struggle. The French ships, however, were well armed with cannon capable of inflicting considerable damage and manned with large crews carrying pistols and swords, hence an unarmed crew would not be able to offer more than token resistance. The report of the capture of a ship in Cromarty in February 1709, given in Appendix IV, shows the effective methods used by the crew of one privateer. It is an indication of the extent of privateering activity that the French naval authorities issued pre-printed blank forms of agreement to their masters. A translation of the form which was signed by Forrester and shown in Figure 25 is set out below (AC 9/402).

'We, the undersigned, Jacques Dunet, captain of the vessel L'Irondelle and Jean fforster, master of the vessel, Helene de Lite [Leith] belonging to Gorge Wanderasme citizen of Eyemouth in Scotland, carrying [or weighing] 40 tonnes. On the 13th April, 1710, sailing from Eyemouth in Scotland to Newcastle under the Danish flag and passport of England and loaded with 6 lasts of fish in barrels belonging to Gorge Wanderasme, citizen of Eyemouth, I agree to ransom the said vessel for the sum of 180 pounds sterling for which I have freed the said vessel to go to the port of Newcastle, where it will be kept for returning under the terms and within 15 days. After the expiry of these terms the present agreement cannot be guaranteed to be taken up by another ship-owner. As security of the ransom I have received as a hostage Jean fforster, captain of the said vessel. All friends and allies are requested to allow free and safe passage of the Helene to proceed to the port of Newcastle without let or hindrance under the stated terms and on the stated route, during the 15 days following.

And I, Jean fforster the aforementioned captain, both in my own name and in that of the aforementioned Gorge Wanderasme, owners of the aforementioned vessel and its cargo, voluntarily give myself up against payment of the aforementioned ransom of the stated sum as guarantor of which I have given the aforementioned captain as hostage, promising not to contravene the terms of the present agreement of which each of us has acquired a copy, which we have signed, having received the captain as hostage. Completed on board the vessel L'Irondelle the 16th April, 1710.

This ransom note in blank has been delivered to Captain Jacques Dunet, master of the Barque L'Irondelle, commissioned in Corsica, by myself clerk of the Admiralty of Calais, signed this 5th day of April, 1710.'

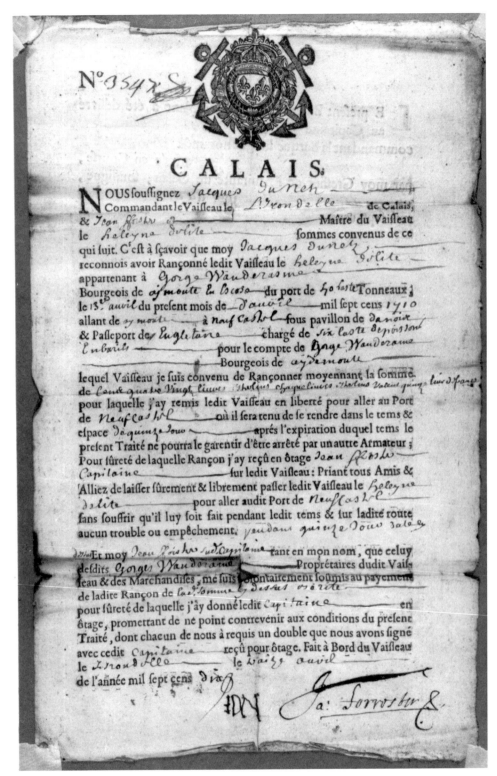

Figure 25   Ransom form of agreement. AC9/402. Reproduced by kind permission of the Keeper of the Records of Scotland.

This final paragraph (above) is on the reverse side of the pre-printed form.

A shipmaster's authority to act on behalf of his owners was recognised by the common law of the sea and by the Scottish courts, and in signing the document Forrester was legally binding his owners to pay the ransom. This same law also recognised that privateers acting with the authority of their country could seize vessels and either sink or take possession of the ships. Privateers could also enter into an agreement with the master of the enemy ship that a ransom be paid so that the ship would be able to continue on her voyage. Masters would of course have signed under duress, a situation which would have made any other agreement invalid. It was accepted that an authorised privateer master was acting lawfully in taking a ransom and therefore giving up his rights to sink or take possession of the ship, and such agreements were accepted as legal documents by the courts (Petrie p. 103).

Some of the statements made in the Form of Agreement deserve explanation.

40 lasts tonneaux. A last was equivalent to 2 tons so this makes the tonnage of the ship 80. A Survey of Scottish owned ships of 15 tons and over carried out in 1710 by the English Board of Customs as part of a reorganisation of the Scottish Custom Service records the tonnage of the *Helen* as 70 tons burthen or 100 measured tons.

The cargo of six lasts or twelve tons of fish was stored in 72 barrels.

...to allow free and safe passage, to proceed without let or hindrance under the stated terms and on the stated route during the 15 days follows. This clause ensured that if the ship was boarded by another privateer within the stated time it could not be kept or ransomed. The number of days allowed for the ship to reach her destination was very generous, even allowing for headwinds and bad weather.

Each privateer master was granted a commission by the French Admiralty and their activities were monitored to ensure that their operations were effective in disrupting the maritime trade of the English and the Scots. There was an additional incentive for the French in their control over the activities of these ships as they obtained a share of the value of each ship ransomed or sold, as did the master of the privateer. The registration number for this particular voyage is given on the top left-hand corner of the Form. The most significant feature of the form is the difference between the writing in the blank spaces which was done by an educated person and the shaky initials of Jacques Dunet which are those of a man who was obviously unable even to write his own name. Jacques Dunet was a Scots Jacobite called James Dunet who, like so many of his compatriots, could not write French and one of his officers would have had the task of completing the form. A considerable number of Jacobites were masters of privateers both during the Nine Years War and in the present conflict, having been granted commissions by James VII and the French naval authorities (Whiteman Bromley and Dickson, p. 35). They adopted French names so that they could claim if captured that they were French citizens acting with the authority of their government. If captured by the English

Navy they were taken to London, tried and hanged, regardless of their nationality and commission. These men would have been experienced masters and employed by the French for their knowledge of the Scottish coast and the trade carried out by the various ports. The privateers that patrolled the coast in 1710 were mainly small vessels which would not stand out from normal traffic and therefore were capable of taking ships by surprise. Being well-armed and able to seize larger ships, they were an effective deterrent to coastal trading.

While the *Helen* carried on trading with her new master, the future for James Forrester, prisoner in Calais, looked bleak. He knew that once the ship was in the possession of its owners they could very likely ignore their obligations to honour the agreement with the French that had been made by their late master and that he would remain in prison until the end of the war, unless the ransom was paid. His only hope of action lay with his wife, Janet Johnston, who in the documents of this case is recorded by her maiden name followed by the description, wife or factrix. It is very unlikely that Forrester would have been able to communicate with his wife when in prison and his wife, who would have stayed in Prestonpans or one of the neighbouring ports, would have been told of the capture by Forth shipmasters who were in Eyemouth when the *Helen* returned to that port. Janet Johnston, who must have been a woman of some character, would have realised that she had to go to Eyemouth to ascertain if the owners were prepared to pay the ransom and the subsistence charges (the French charged captured seaman 2s 6d per day for the pleasure of staying in their prisons).

James Forrester was not a part owner of the ship, as he is described in court records as being an input master, a term used to describe a master who did not have shares in his ship. From a statement made in the subsequent court case the owners apparently told Janet that as her husband had no authority from them to ransom the ship it was his responsibility to find the money required to obtain his freedom. They did, however, give her the derisory sum of £5 as a contribution towards his subsistence expenses.

Janet Johnston was not the only woman to have difficulty in obtaining money from owners so that her husband's ransom could be paid. In 1711 Elizabeth Enden took an action to free her husband, David Tod, mariner in the *Nonsuch* (the master being John Hay), after the vessel was captured by a French privateer and Tod given as hostage for the ransom. In a petition to the Admiralty Court it was stated that she had 'entreated him [Hay] to see to the releasing of my husband by procuring his ransom… yet he slights and mocks me, and tells me my husband was a fool for giving pledge'. The petition requested that Hay be imprisoned and the ship arrested (AC 10/108).

The problem of obtaining money to pay for a ransom was not confined to wives. In 1706 John Corson, skipper of Crail, pursued George Blyth, skipper of West Wemyss, for the ransom of his son William who was given as hostage when Blyth's ship, the *Fortune of Wemyss,* was taken by a privateer, the *Deana* of Dunkirk, returning from Trondheim (AC 9/190). There are several cases of a similar nature in

Admiralty Court records of this period, and no doubt there were other occasions when men were ransomed and the money paid by the owners albeit with difficulty but without the necessity of going to court.

Because of the known threat of privateers, James Forrester would have requested from the owners instruction on how he should deal with a demand for ransom and it was claimed by Forrester that one of the owners did give him such instructions. An example of the nature of the instructions supplied to masters are those given to Nicoll Young, skipper of *The Elizabeth* of Findhorn by Kirkcaldy merchants in April 1696. One of these merchants, James Ross, travelled to Findhorn to negotiate the purchase of the cargo and he would have ensured that Young carried out the following instruction (Seton p. 253–57).

> 'If it should fall out, as God forbid, yt you should be tucke by a french privitier, then and in y uncaise, you sall goe y lenthe of four hundredthe pounds Scotts for ransom of y meall and bear; but I hop you sall doe it cheaper. And, in cais it be that ye master be unwilling to ransome his shippe, then we allow you to pay y lenth of fiftie pound sterling money, qch we oblidg ourselves to pay, bill upon sight.'

When Janet Johnston returned home she decided that her only course of action was to engage a lawyer to raise an action in the Admiralty Court to make the owners pay the ransom and subsistence charges.

As stated earlier, Janet Johnston would have known that her husband could apply to the Court for permission to have his ship sold in order to pay any debts incurred by him in the course of his employment. This right also extended to freight earned by the ship. In addition, the law recognised that the owners of a ship were bound to pay any ransom agreed by the master of their ship. She would have found the prospect of going to the Admiralty Court a daunting one. Apart from being the only woman in the Court, she would be dependent upon the effectiveness of her lawyer and that she was not acting in her own right but as a judicial factor. The defendants in the case were George Windram of Eyemouth, William Hodge of Hardcarse, George Hume of Whitfield and his brother Alex Hume, all men of property and capable of putting forward a good defence. Janet Johnston's claim that the *Helen* be rouped (sold by auction) was agreed by the Court and, as was the practice, an inventory of the ship was prepared.

The sale of the ship to John Mathie, a Prestonpans merchant and shipmaster, realised the sum of £101 after meeting expenses of £13. This sum was insufficient to meet the cost of the ransom of £180 sterling (AC 9/400).

At a further meeting of the Court in January 1711 when objections to the sale were raised by the owners, it was agreed that both parties would submit their case under oath and in the meantime the Court stated that the ship must be rouped. The Defendants' lawyer then submitted the following defence.

And they do allege that they ought not to be liable, nor their shares of the said ship affected, with the reason because he had no commission from the said defenders or any of the owners to ransom the ship. Yea, upon the contrary was discharged to ransom her in case of capture. Which if need be shall be instructed by a missive letter under the hostager's own hand, in Eyemouth's [George Windram] custody.

Secondly, the hostage having taken upon to ransom without warrant, the defenders conceive they cannot be further liable than conform to their shares of the ship ransomed which, though they be not obliged, they are content to give up, and are satisfied that the ship be rouped for payment of the ransom. Which they do out of mere pity and commiseration. But they humbly conceive they cannot be personally liable, the ransom being not only unwarrantable, but likewise the sum agreed far exceeding the value of the ship and goods, which was likewise very foolish. And they would rather that the ship and goods have been burnt than ransom her at such an extravagant rate.

Janet Johnston acting as factrix on behalf of her husband then submitted the following answers to the above defence.

The said James Forrester being input master of the said ship in a voyage from Eyemouth to Newcastle where he was to take in coals &c fro the defender's behoof and was to transport these with the other goods put aboard at Eyemouth to Hamburg and there to take in such goods as they should order and from thence to sail to Norway and there to take in timber and other goods to be put aboard there and to return to Eyemouth. When the ship had sailed but two leagues from Eyemouth in the voyage to Newcastle, the same was seized by a French privateer and thereafter ransomed for £180 sterling, for which the said James Forrester went hostage, and the owners and freighters having failed in payment of the ransom and most cruelly suffered him to lie prisoner at Calais, therefore since the month of March[1] last he is obliged to raise a process against the owners and freighters of the said ship for payment of the said ransom and his damages and expenses.

The defences given in the said process are that the prisoner had no order to ransom and that therefore the defenders cannot be personally liable, but only obliged to give up their interests in the said ship and cargo aboard at the time, which they accordingly do give up.

It's answered first; That it's still entire and competent for the pursuer(s) to prove by their oaths that they or either of them, particularly Eyemouth [George Windram] who employed him in the name of the rest, gave him orders to ransom, which must make him liable for the sum libelled. But secondly et seperatim it is not sufficient for the defenders to give up their interest in the terms they offered because they have since the ransoming owned the ship and legal the pursuer's management in ransoming the same, and have since the seizure unloaded and put aboard goods at the several parts owners. And particularly the Laird of Eyemouth and Robertson went to Newcastle immediately after the ransoming and put aboard coals and goods for themselves and partners, and ordered out the ship in prosecution of the voyage, and they now disingenuously deny all asset. They so far owned the grounds of the pursuer's libel at first, that they remitted, as they themselves pretend, five pounds sterling for his aliment. Thirdly; not only the ship but also the several cargoes aboard the said ship since the seizure and sold and intrometted with by them or for their behoof. As also the product thereof and freights of the said ship, ought to be applied for the sums libelled, seeing all followed in prosecution of the voyage wherein the ship was seized and ransomed. And in so far as the intromission extent of the said cargoes, freights etc shall not be proven by bills of lading, invoices and other writs relative thereto, in the defenders their own hands (which they ought to exhibit upon oath) the same offered to be proven by their oaths of verity.

In addition to the above statement Janet Johnston provided the following details of her husband's damages and expenses in pounds Scots (AC 9 402).

Accompt of damage and expenses due to James Forrester... by the owners & freighters of the Helen of Leith

	£	s	d
Impr. Consultations to end ...	12	18	0
To by ...	4	10	0
To a petition given in herewith	0	12	10
To the Extract of the Deed	30	00	0
To the hostage's charges and expenses at Calais from the tenth day of April 1710 to the first of June 1711 at half a crown per diem	555	00	0
To his expenses homeward	60	00	0
	£663	00	10

At that time a pound sterling was equivalent to £12 Scots so the above total was equal to £55 sterling. This statement was prepared in January 1711 and the claim for expenses is based on James Forrester being freed on 1st June, 1711. The lawyer was taking into account the length of time for judgement to be pronounced and the time required to negotiate with the French and transfer the ransom money and the prison expenses. On 20th March the Court found the Defendants liable and a cautioner appointed on behalf of Janet Johnston on 3rd April.

* Some words in this document are not entirely legible.

Janet Johnston then approached John Mathie to act as her cautioner. This meant that Mathie would become responsible for ensuring that the owners paid £134 to Janet Johnston and that he would ensure that Janet Johnston applied this sum and the proceeds of the roup for payment of the ransom and expenses. A bond of caution was entered into on 3rd April 1711 and an extract is given below.

> *And decerned therefore, the pursuer's factrix finding caution before extract[1] to apply the same for payment of the ransom and charges towards his liberation. Therefore to be bound and obliged. Likewise I bind and oblige me, my heirs, executors and successors, as caution and surety acted in the books of the High Court of Admiralty. That the said Janet Johnston shall apply for foresaid sum of one hundred and thirtyfour pounds sterling, when received of the persons a[fore]named found liable therin a manner a[fore]eften* towards payment of the foresaid ransom and charges, and relieving the said James Forrester, and that she shall not otherwise dispose of the same, nor no part thereof for any other use whatsoever.*

It is significant that John Mathie was chosen to act as guarantor by the Court because as a merchant he would have been in a position to know which merchant houses had dealings with French merchants (to ensure that the sum due to the French would be transferred). Although the two countries were at war, monies due to one nation or the other were apparently transferred without too much difficulty. The agents were in some cases the established Franco-Irish business houses who had been based in several French ports since Cromwell's action in Ireland in 1649/50. A considerable number of seamen were ransomed during the Nine Years War and the present conflict, and the transfer of money due for ransom and subsistence would have been done by British and French merchant houses who had considerable experience in these transactions and had maintained good relations with British merchants during the war (Whiteman Bromley and Dickson, p. 22–3).

A subsequent case involved the sale of the *Helen*. The vessel was purchased by John Mathie, complete with rigging, sails and all equipment, for £115. He later raised an action in the same Admiralty Court to recover rigging, sails, ensign and sundry equipment included in the inventory prior to the roup and found to be missing when he took possession. He valued the missing equipment, no doubt at replacement cost, at £158 8s 0d and requested that the previous owners replace the missing items. Unfortunately, no record exists of the decision of the Court (AC 10/114).

There is no mention of James Forrester nor of Janet Johnston in Admiralty Court records after 1711 and, as port records do not exist for a considerable period after 1711, it is not possible to ascertain whether Forrester returned to Scotland and was thereafter employed as master of a ship.

---

* Some words in this document are not entirely legible.

[1] Although the document states March this is obviously incorrect and was an error by the lawyer preparing the Defence.

Bibliography

Adair, John, 1703. *A Description of the Sea Coast and Islands of Scotland.*

Baker, Wm. A. 1983. *The Mayflower & Other Colonial Vessels.* London, Conway Maritime Press, pp. 126–143.

Clark, Alex, 1911. *A Short History of the Shipmaster Society.* Aberdeen, Wm. Smith & Sons.

Collins, Greenvile, 1693. *Great Britain's Coastal Pilot.*

Cowan, I.B. and Shaw, D. (Eds.) 1993. *The Renaissance or Reformation in Scotland.* Article by Margaret H.B. Sanderson, p. 182–199.

Cunliffe, Tom, 1988. *Topsails and Battleaxe.* Devon, David & Charles.

Dobson, David, 1993. *The Mariners of the Lothians 1600–1700;*

Dobson, David, 1992. *The Mariners of Kirkcaldy & West Fife 1600–1700.*

Davis, Ralph, 1962. *The Rise of the English Shipping Industry.* London, MacMillan & Co. Ltd.

Duckham, B.F., 1970. *A History of the Scottish Coal Industry 1700–1815.* Newton Abbot, David & Charles.

Finch, R., 1973. *Coals from Newcastle.* Suffolk, Terence Dalton Ltd.

Fury, C.A., 1999. The Training and Education in the Elizabethan Maritime Community. *Mariners Mirror,* **85**; 147–161.

Graham, Angus, 1968-69. Archaeological Notes on some Harbours in Eastern Scotland. *Proceedings of Society of Antiquaries of Scotland,* **101**; 200–285.

Graham, E.J., 1992. In Defence of the Scottish Maritime Interest, *Scottish Historical Review,* **192**; 88–109.

Grant, James, 1914. *The Old Scots Navy.* London, Naval Records Society.

Gurney, Alan, 1997. *Below the Convergence.* New York, N.N. Norton.

Hatcher, John, 1993. *The History of the British Coal Industry Before 1700.* Vol I, Oxford Clarendon Press.

Hutchison, G., 1994. *Medieval Ships & Shipping.* London, Leicester University Press.

Inglis, H.R.G., 1918. *John Adair: An Early Mapmaker and His Work. Scottish Geographi-*

cal Magazine, **34**; 60–66.

Marwick, Hugh, 1939. *Merchant Lairds of Long Ago*. Kirkwall.

Marwick, J.D., 1881. *Records of Convention of Royal Burghs 1677–1711*. Edinburgh, Scottish Burgh Records Society.

May, W.E., 1973. *A History of Marine Navigation*. London, Foulis.

Mowat, Sue, 1994. *The Port of Leith*. Edinburgh, John Murray.

Neff, J.U., 1966. *The Rise of the British Coal Industry*. Vol 2, Appendix C, London, Frank Cass & Co.

Oertling, Thomas J., 1996. *Ships' Bilge Pumps*. Texas A & M University Press.

Petrie, Donald, 1993. The Ransoming of Eliza Swan. *American Neptune*, **53**(2); 48–108.

Robinson, A.H.W., 1958. The Charting of the Scottish Coasts. *Scottish Geographical Magazine*, **74**; 166–167.

Salisbury, William, 1964. Early Tonnage Measurement in England. Mariner's Mirror, **52**; 41–51; **53**; 69–75.

Salisbury, William, 1936. Merchantmen in 1754. *Mariner's Mirror*, **22**; 346–353.

Seton, B., 1921. A Seventeenth Century Deal in Corn. *Scottish Historical Review*, **18**; 253–256.

Smith, John, 1970. *A Sea Grammar.* Edited by K. Goell, London, Michael Joseph.

Smout, T.C., 1963. *Scottish Trade on the Eve of Union*. Edinburgh, Oliver & Boyd.

Taylor, L.B., 1972. *Aberdeen Shore Work Accounts 1596-1670*. Aberdeen University Press.

Taylor, E.G.R., 1957. *Cartography Survey & Navigation*. History of Technology. Singer Holmyard, Williams Oxford, Vol II, pp. 482–498.

Taylor, E.G.R. and Richey, M.W., 1962. *The Geometrical Seaman*. Hollis & Carter.

Whatley, C.A., 1987. *The Scottish Salt Industry*. Aberdeen University Press.

Whiteman, A., Bromley, T.S. and Dickson, P.G.M., 1973. *Statesmen, Scholars & Merchants*. Oxford University Press.

Secondary sources

Anstead, A., 1985. *Dictionary of Sea Terms*. Glasgow, Brown Son & Ferguson.

Greenhill, Basil, 1988. *The Evolution of the Wooden Ship*. London, Batsford.

Harland, John, 1984. *Seamanship*. London, Conway Maritime Press.

Lenman, B., 1980. *The Jacobite Rising in Britain 1689–1746*. London, Eyre Methuen.

Sinclair, Sir John, 19XX. *Old Statistical Accounts for Scotland*. Lothians Vol 2; Fife Vol 10.

Tipping, C., 1994. Cargo Handling and the Medieval Log. *Mariner's Mirror*, **80**; 3–15.

Zupko, R.F., 1977. The Weights and Measures of Scotland Before the Union. *Scottish Historical Review*, **56**; 118–145.

Manuscript sources

Edinburgh City Archives

Enactment Book of Leith Baillie Court
   ECA/SL86/3/2

National Archives of Scotland

Records of the High Court of Admiralty
   AC 7/8 8 Feb 1687
   AC 7/9 5 12 1691
   AC 8/87 109
   AC 9/13 1
   AC 9/42 190 321 345 356 377 381 400 402 467
   AC 10/109 114
Customs Outport Records
   Prestonpans E 72/21 15 16 21 22
   Leith E 72/15/45
   Kirkcaldy E 72/9 24 27 28 29
Register House
   RH 9/1 258-260

National Library of Scotland

Rules Orders & Instructions Made & Published by the Commissioners of Customs & Excise in Scotland 1656

Chart of Edinburgh Firth being part of Great Britain's Coasting Pilot prepared by Captain Greenvile Collins 1693

Chart of the Frith of Forth being part of the Description of the Sea Coast and Islands of Scotland by John Adairs

Aberdeen University Library

Records of Convention of Royal Burghs 1677–1711, Account of the Ships of Leith 17th May 1692 p. 56

Description of the Sea Coast and Islands of Scotland by John Adair Page 7 of Vol I

Public Record Office

Capture of an Orkney sloop by a privateer in 1709. PRO, Vol CXIII, No. 43.

Appendix 1

Transcription of the Disbursements of the George of Port Seton, 1687–1690; James Forrester, Master*

Page one

An account of money paid to my men for their wages from Holland to Norway from the month of March to the last of May in the year 1687, and likewise the expences that I have paid to Mr Alexr Drumand upon the account of the ship.

	£	s	d
Imprimis for myself	80		
to my mate John Banks	40		
to Robert Couan	31	16	
to Patrick Couan	31	16	
to Mark Peddin	31	16	
to William Thomson	20		
to Mr Alexander Droumand	60		
to his man, a new hat for his pains	7	4	
	304	12	

[deleted – paid to John Adair his dues for each voyage I have made since I had the ship, at £2.00 per voyage for eight voyages, which comes to £16 for the Light of May each voyage …]

* extracted by courtesy of Edinburgh City Archives, re. ECA/SL86/3/2

Page two

Account of money disbursed for provisions for the use of my voyage from Cockenzie to Greenock and from thence to Norway and from Norway to the Harbour of Cockenzie, from the month of July '87 to the month of March '88

	£	s	d
for reporting the ship outward	2	16	
6½ ells of sacking to be a tarpaulin for the main hatches	2	6	
to a flesher for killing 2 swine		14	
for dressing 2 lamps		12	
2 horns for the night house (binnacle)		3	
John Mudie for 7 days work @ £1 4s per day	8	8	
1 stone oakum	1	7	
for anchorage and for trimming my beer and water casks	1	7	
for ten days of a pitch pot; each day 2s	1		
for fresh fish		14	
Francis Davidson for 2 swine	10		
to him for 4cwt of bread at £5 14s per 100	22	16	
Robert Gilmore for a swine	9		
William Brown for a swine	7	4	
William Leslie for nails	9		
William Sanderson for 3 pecks groats	2	8	
half a boll of peas [1.25cwt]	3	6	8
Widow Balfour for beer	6		
2½ doz dry fish	5	12	
James Trotter for meat and drink to the men and boys			
in time of livering and loading the ship	26	12	
drink given to the metters and boatmen			
to take care of the salt	1	12	
George Seton for an oak plank	1	16	
Jasper Knoules for 1 stone of candles	3	4	
Robert Seton for 1 boll [2.5cwt] of meal	5		
to the Collector at giving in bound for the salt		19	
2¼ stone of butter	6	14	
ten lasts of ballast [?120 barrels]	9	10	
16 stone of beef @ 21s per stone	16	16	
for my Coket at Port Glasgow	2	8	
John Adair his dues at 1s per tun; 40 tuns	2		
for my report outward at Greenock	1	8	
3 tierces of beer	15	6	8
2 handspikes		12	
	189	2	8

The George of Port Seton

	£	s	d
The sum of the other side brought over, which is	*189*	*2*	*8*
a half vat of beer	2		
6 gall of ale	4	10	
6 last of ballast	2	16	
1 barrel of tar	6		
an empty tar barrel to black the ship		6	
1 doz dry fish	3		
2 pump stop and a bucket	1	4	
8 lasts of ballast	4	4	
2 pecks of groats	1	13	4
4 loads of peats		18	
an empty tierce, for water	1		
for baking a boll of meal		16	
a side of mutton		18	
a piece of oak to make to chestrees		14	
for a carpenter to finish the same		18	
2 iron bolts for the same		8	
300 fresh herrings	1	4	
4lb candles	1		
2 loads of peats		9	
for my Gold Penny ticket		9	
[gold penny @ 3s per ton = 60 tons?]			

Follows expenses in the Lewis

	£	s	d
2 doz dried fish	4	16	
a cow	10		
to the man that slew her		4	
2 loads of peats		6	

Follows expenses in Orkney

	£	s	d
half one hundred biscuit	3		
a boll of meal	5	6	8
6 gal of beer	2	8	

Follows expenses in Shetland

	£	s	d
a hawser, 90 fathoms long	18		
a barrel of fish	6		
¼ of a cow	1	9	

	£	s	d
a whole cow	8	6	
a small ox	5		
2 great oxen	23		
3 chopins of lamp oil		18	
2 beef barrels	2		
7 fresh keeling		14	

Page four

	£	s	d
the sum of the other two sides brought over which is	323	6	8
a pilot at Shetland	2	18	
an empty beef barrel	1		
39lb great salt for salting our beef		18	
a teirce of beer	4	12	
104lb of meal	4	16	
for baking a boll of meal		14	
a boat full of peats		12	

Follows expenses at Norway

	£	s	d
6 handspikes and 2 capstan bars	1		
fresh fish	5	12	
ships beer	7		
bread	11		
8lb candles	2		
lamp oil		5	
for heading 2 beef barrels		5	
33lb butter	3	17	
half a barrel of fish	4	4	
bread	5	12	
beer	2	2	
peas and groats	1	16	
one firkin salt mackerel	1	18	
bread	3	16	
a boat full of wood		7	
expenses going from the Brimmell Haven to Alexander Dick's for bread	1	8	
4lb butter		10	
a boat to go to Bergen to buy provisions		12	
my own expenses and my mens' for going to Bergen	4	4	
for bread bought there	4	4	

	£	s	d
half a barrel of peas	3	4	
a can of lamp oil		10	
cabbage		14	
wood		6	
100 fresh herrings		7	
a firkin salt fish	1	8	

Page five

the sum of the other 3 sides brought over, which is	406	1	8

E. penses at Fraserburgh

	£	s	d
½ stone butter	1	8	
anchorage	1	3	4
for reporting the ship	1	10	
2 tierces beer	8		
peats		12	
1 pt lamp oil		10	
fresh fish	1	4	
a side of pork	2	10	
2 pecks peas		12	
1 peck groats		12	
to a doctor for curing the boy's foot	1	8	
3½ doz salt fish		18	
pilotage in and out of Fraserburgh	3	4	

Expenses at Glasgow

	£	s	d
2lb twine for our sails		12	
24 ells vitrie for mending the sails	5	10	
for dressing the compasses	1	10	
a half hour glass		8	
sail needles		10	
1cwt bread	7		
a sounding lead line	3	10	
for carrying them from Glasgow to Greenock			
my own expenses from Greenock to Seton to get my freight, and for my horse hire	12		
1/3 of average, conform to charter party	5	16	
my extraordinary expenses in terms of the voyage	12		
for my mens wages			
imprimis for myself	80		

	£	s	d
John Banks	40		
Robert Couan	32		
Patrick Couan	32		
William Thomson	33		
George Pedin	18		
Mark Pedin	16		

Expenses in Cockenzie

	£	s	d
for reporting the ship inward	2	18	
for my sufferance		12	
for entering the ship		12	
meat and drink to the fishermen			
for helping us in to the harbour	7	5	
3 days of a man to help unload the ship		18	

Page six

An account of money received for my freight for the said voyage from New Port Seton to Greenock and from Greenock to Norway and from thence to Port Seton, from the month of July '87 to the month of March 1688

Freight for 52 chalders of salt at 6 dollars per chalder	£904	16s
Charges	£743	4s
Profit	£161	12s

Page seven

An account of money disbursed for the use of my voyage from New Port Seton to London, with 51 chalders of salt on the account of the noble Earl of Winton, from the month of May to the first of July 1688

	£	s	d
2 barrels of tar for dressing the ship	16	12	
carpenters for 22 days work at £1 sc per day	22		
1 stone oakum	1	6	8
an anchor and an anchor stock and for stocking it	28	4	
for nails and one pair of termenters (purpose unknown)	14	12	

The George of Port Seton

	£	s	d
for building our hearth	1	12	
deals and trees to build the fore room	11	12	
500lb biscuit @ £5 14s per 100	22	16	
2 tierces beer and 2 × 6gal barrels of ale	15	4	
6 swine	43	8	
3 legs beef	14		
6 pecks groats and half boll of peas	6	4	
2 threaves of wheat straw for brimming [?burning] the ship	1	8	
meat and drink to the carpenters and boys in time			
of lying in the harbour	30		
anchorage	1	3	4
drink to my men in time of loading	1	9	6
12lb candles	2	8	
a pump box, and for carrying a barrel of tar from the Pans		16	
half a dozen dried fish and a quarter of butter	2	3	
4 hens for my passengers	1	8	
reporting the ship outward	1	8	
to the fishermen for helping out the ship		16	
fresh fish bought at sea	6	12	
for trimming our beer and water cask	1	14	
7 ells sacking to be a tarpaulin for the main hatches	2	9	
12 days use of a pitch pot @ 2s sc per day	1	4	

London disbursements [in margin]

	£	s	d
reporting the ship at London	3	7	
light money	6	1	
an anchor stock	4	16	
½ firking of butter	6		
35 tuns ballast	18		
100 and ¼ of ropes @ £16 4s per 100	20	5	
foul butter for the masts and blocks		12	
for dressing the compasses and the glasses,			
and for a hand lead and 4 black boxes	5	17	
2 skeins of marlin		12	

<u>Page eight</u>

	£	s	d
blocks and sheaves	1	18	
1cwt bread	4	10	
80lb fresh beef	6	12	
soft bread for the passengers, and green peas	1		
a pewter basin for the ship's use	1	16	

	£	s	d
for beer and wharfage	[	]	
for putting my bills on the Exchange at London and Edr	2	4	
for getting out my cokets	12	14	
for the broker that gives them in and gets them out	7	4	
for clearing at Gravesend	9	12	
to the gunner of the fort		6	
for my mens wages;			
imprimis to myself	66		
the mate, John Banks	42		
William Thomson	22	16	
Alexander Mudie	22	16	
Robert Couan	22	16	
Jasper Knouls	22	16	
Patrick Couan	22	16	
for my extraordinary expenses for procuring			
passengers and goods	12		
a sheep for my passengers	3	14	
for my report inwards and my sufferance	3	10	
meat and drink to my men and boys in time of livering	6		
for an Admiral's pass	12		

Page nine

An account of money received of freight for the forsaid voyage from New Port Seton to London and thence home to Port Seton, from the month of May to the month of July in the year 1688.

for 51 chalders salt the freight is	360
freight of 18 barrels of eggs at £1 per barrel	18
freight of pack goods	12
for passengers	48

For goods and passengers from London

for Gofford's corps	144
for goods and passengers	84

Freight   £666
Charges   £620 10s 6d
Profit   £45 10s 6d

The George of Port Seton

Account of disbursements for the use of my voyage from New Port Seton to London with 51 chalders of salt on the account of the Earl of Winton from the month of July to the last of September in the year 1688

	£	s	d
For reporting the ship outward	1	8	
for carrying out my ballast	2		
2½ days of a carpenter, each day £1	2	10	
for trimming our beer and water cask	1	18	
1 tierce and 2 × ½ hogshead of beer	10		
3 barrels of beef	46	10	
4 pecks of groats	2	13	4
3 firlots peas	3	15	
½ stone of candles	1	12	
to the fishermen for helping the ship out of the harbour		16	
for reporting the ship at London	3	7	
for light money	6	1	
for putting my bill on the Exchange		18	
for my pump box		14	
210lb biscuit	12	11	
a pump staff	1	8	
2 pr of bands and 100 window nails		12	
200 door nails, 200 plansher nails, 200 scupper nails	2	16	
19lb ropes	2	18	
a fish hook for our anchor		16	
35 tuns ballast	18		
7½ lb foul butter for the masts		15	
2½ cwt of biscuit	11	5	
a lantern		18	
ships beer	21		
for getting my cokets out	11	8	
for clearing at Gravesend	9	18	
fresh meat and 3lb butter	10	6	
4lb candles		18	
2 gimlets for the ship's use		4	
for repairing my 2 mainsails	33	6	
to the fishermen to help in the ship to the harbour	1	2	
paid for damage done by us to an Englishman at London	21	12	

Page ten

for my mens wages;			
imprimis to myself	66		

	£	s	d
my mate John Banks	42		
Alexander Mudie	22	16	
William Thomson	22	16	
Robert Couan	22	16	
Patrick Couan	22	16	
Jasper Knouls	22	16	

	£	s	d
for my extraordinary expenses procuring goods and passengers	6		
for putting my bill on the Exchange at Edinburgh		14	
for reporting the ship inward at Prestonpans and for my sufferance	3	12	
for drink to my men in time of livering the ship	1	4	
to Murdie Mackloud for looking after the ship in time of lying in the harbour	2	7	
anchorage	1	3	4

An account of money received in freight for the forsaid voyage from New Port Seton to London and from thence home to Port Seton from the month of July to the last of September in the year 1688

	£	s	d
for the freight of 62 weighs of salt at 8s 6d ster per weigh, which is in Scots money	316	4	
15 barrels of eggs	15		
other goods	4		
2 passengers	8	8	

For goods and passengers from London

	£	s	d
freight of goods	45	17	
for passengers	46	4	

Freight   £435 13s

Charges   £487 11s 4d

Loss   £41 8s 4d

Page eleven

An account of money disbursed for the use of my voyage from New Port Seton to Rotterdam with a load of small coal on the account of James Smith in Tranent and James Watt in Prestonpans, for the month of October to the first of December in the year 1688

The George of Port Seton

	£	s	d
For carrying out my ballast	3	6	
a barrel of tar	8	4	
nails	3	6	
2 carpenters, 4½ days	8	10	
3 barrels of beef and carrying it to Port Seton	37	18	
beer	10	10	
for trimming our beer and water cask		14	
for a swine	9		
2cwt of bread	10	16	
4 pecks of groats	2	16	
half a boll of peas	2	10	
anchorage	1	3	4
ale for the stousters [?stowsters/stowers] and the bearers	1	4	
the fishermen for helping the ship out	1	10	
James Trotter for meat and drink for the carpenter and boys	12	15	
for my coket*	1		
a stone of candles	3	4	
1lb twine		8	
a pass from Council	2	6	
for my pilotage over the Mase and from the Briell to Rotterdam	28	12	
to the pilots for getting my cable and anchor again at the Pit	14		
1 doz cabbage	1	1	
a beer kann		4	
1lb butter		7	
half a barrel of herring	4	12	
for mending our hearth	4	8	
for a new jib	28	6	
64lb ropes	8	6	
anchorage in Holland	1	6	
20 last of ballast	15	15	
beer	15	9	
bread	10	1	
a bottle of train [whale] oil for the lamps	1	18	
4lb candles	1	1	4
for damage	1	3	
pilotage over the Mase homeward	1	16	
for helping the ship into the harbour		16	

* James Forrester was not concerned with the spelling of the word used to describe this document and used the term 'coket' when recording payment of the fee.

	£	s	d

<u>Page twelve</u>

	£	s	d
for postage, searight and lightage	6	14	
for beaconage and bouage [bouyage?] inward	3	12	
for writing my passport	1	16	
for beaconage and bouage outward	3	12	
to the Job Master for taxing the ship	1	8	
last money; 26 last at 15 stivers [390 stivers]	21	16	
to the waiters for subscribing my passport			
for my mens wages;		14	
imprimis for myself	44		
John Banks, mate	22	18	
Alexander Mudie	16	16	
Thomas Turnbull	16	16	
William Thomson	16	16	
John Lokert	16	16	
Murdie Mackloud	14		
George Cowan	10		

An account of money received of freight for the forsaid voyage from New Port Seton to Rotterdam and so home, for the last of October to the last of December in the year 1688

	£	s	d
freight of 47 hoods 3½ sacks at 5Gl and 15s per hood, which is in Scots money	302	13	8
freight of 2 hogsheads lintseed	2		
freight of 10,000 trees for the Earl of Winton	6		

Freight   £310 13s 8d
Charges £455 15s 8d
Loss   £145 2s

<u>Page Thirteen</u>

An account of money disbursed for the use of my voyage from Elphinstone to Rotterdam with a lading of great coal from 1 April '89 to the last of June 1689

	£	s	d
2 barrels of tar	19		
2 stone of roset [rosin]	2	6	8
Robert Ballinton for iron work	2		4
to the carpenters	20		
a new bittikell	4		
for horns to the same		16	

The George of Port Seton

	£	s	d
for helping out the ship	1	8	
for reporting the ship at Bo'ness	1	8	
[Bo'ness – in margin]			
half an anker of ale		16	8
half a hundred biscuit	2	18	
a tierce of beer	3	6	8
ale at Elphinstone		19	
1½ threaves of wheat straw	4		
iron work at Elphinstone		19	
half a boll of beans	2	16	8
4 pecks groats	3	4	
6 swine	39	16	
1 ox	14		
half a barrel of beef	7		
for carrying 3 barrels of beef and pork to the harbour		12	
400lb bread at £5 8s per 100	21	12	
nails	7	18	
1 stone candles	3	4	
2 tierces and 2 half hogsheads of beer	14		
expenses of carrying my/me up the water	3		
for mending the kettle		10	6
1lb pump lader/leather		14	
2 shovels	1	16	
fresh fish at sea		15	
for mending the bucket		3	
Anchorage at Cockenzie	1	3	4
James Trotter for meat and drink to the carpenters and boys	46		

Page Fourteen

[margin – expenses in Holland]	£	s	d
avarage, conform to charter party	17	3	
new ropes	8		
32lb old ropes	2	14	8
blocks	1	13	
3 scaepers/scrapers	1	13	6
shoredues	1	7	
mending my topsail	5	18	
dressing the compasses and glasses and for a new vane	2		
2lb twine	11	6	

	£	s	d
40 sail needles		7	
fresh fish		7	
hammer slaugh/haugh to the deck (purpose unknown)		4	6
green bread	7	4	4
paint and oil	4	1	4
2½ stoups vinegar		11	6
20 lasts ballast	15	10	4
beer	29	16	
for the mens welcome to Rotterdam	3	7	
my part of convoy money, to the Jeuish/Irish* frigate	43	18	4
for mending the rudder pin at the Briell	2	4	8
to the Commisar's boatmen at the Briell		11	
a half barrel of beer	2		4
green bread	1	18	8
to the men of the potaesh*		7	
for my sailing orders, to the captain of the man-of-war	2		
for fresh fish at sea		10	
for helping the ship into the harbour		16	
for my mens wages;			
John Banks, mate	22	12	
Thomas Turnbull	16	16	
Patrick Couan	16	16	
Alexander Mudie	16	16	
Robert Couan	16	16	
Jasper Knoulls	16	16	
Murdie Mackloud	14	14	
my own wages	44	16	
2 firelocks for the ship and powder for the same	8	8	

Page Fifteen

An account of money received for freight for the forsaid voyage from Elphinstone to Rotterdam from 1 April '89 to the last of June 1689

	£	s	
hud 8¾ great coal at 30 G per 100; the freight by the broker's bill comes to 256 guilders and 6 stivers. After all dues are paid, in Scots money it is	287	1	
freight of 20 barr beef	22	12	
freight homeward, from William Cuthbertson	46		

* wording unclear

113

The George of Port Seton

Freight £355 13s

Charges £570 11s

Loss   £214 18s

<u>Page Sixteen</u>

An account of money disbursed for the use of my voyage from the Wemyss to Campveere with a lading of great coal, from the middle of July to the last of September in the year 1689.

	£	s	d
anchorage at Cockenzie	1	3	4
for helping out the ship from Cockenzie		16	
for helping in the ship to the Wemyss	1	4	
to a carpenter for half a tide's work		7	
ale and beer in time of loading for the sea	15		
to my report outward	1	18	
100lb bread	18		
3 barrels of beef	42		
half a barrel of pork	10		
half a stone of candles	1	10	
to the fishermen for weighing my anchor in the road of Cockenzie	1	4	
meat and drink to my boys men in time of the ship's lying in the harbour of Cockenzie, and for drink to the men	1	4	
to the Captains of the convoy for my sailing orders	3	10	

Expenses at Campveere

	£	s	d
my report		7	
a sack of peas	3	18	
100lb French barley	4		
for bringing them from Middleburgh to Campveere in the wagon		4	6
half a stoup of linseed oil		8	2
2lb yellow paint		4	6
3lb red paint		10	6
nails	3	6	8
for repairing the boat	22	10	8
12 last of ballast	10	4	
2 half hogsheads and 5 half barrels of beer	13	8	6
for dressing the cask		7	

	£	s	d
for mending the sails	2	4	8
for a pilot from Campveere to Rotterdam	12	13	
for expenses by the way	1	2	4

Expenses at Rotterdam

	£	s	d
1 firkin tar	2	16	
78lb rope at 11½ G per 100	10	2	8
a new main topsail of carrea duck containing 97 holland ells at 10¼ stivers per ell	57	14	
line, rebands and marlin for the same	1	8	

Page Seventeen

	£	s	d
a half hogshead and 2 half barrels of beer	7		
haven dues	1	13	6
my passport outward from Rotterdam, for buidge and lightage	7	16	6
10lb roset	1	2	4
2 bushells peas	3	5	
4 brooms		4	6
25lb piligarst (purpose not known)	1		
cabbage		14	
20lb fresh beef	2	4	8
for a pu[t] up lantern	2	14	
paid to the customs boat at the Briell		14	
to the potashes boat		14	
for my sailing orders	3	10	
for my part of the Captains' reckoning	1	13	6
for my mens wages;			
Adam Burnett, mate	30	4	
Thomas Turnbull	22	8	
William Thomson	22	8	
Murdie Mackloud	21		
to myself	46		
for average at Campveere	4	14	
hiring 3 men to load our ship for dispatch	3	10	

The George of Port Seton

An account of money received for the forsaid freight from the Wemyss to
Campveere in the forsaid months of the year 1689

	£	s	d
freight of 900 and a quarter great coal at 35 guilders and 15 stivers per 100, which is in Scots money	362	1	
freight homeward	6		

Freight £368 1s

Charges £448 9s 8d

Loss   £80 8s 8d

An account of money disbursed for the use of my voyage from Port Seton to
London for the 1 November 1689 to the middle of April 1690

	£	s	d
anchorage at Cockenzie	1	3	4
a plank; 26ft × 22in × 2 ½ in	9	10	
my expenses in going to Leith to buy it, and for horse hire	1	4	
for bringing it from Leith to Port Seton	1	10	
David Durie, carpenter, for 8 days at £1 4s per day	9	12	
his man for 8 days at £1 per day	8		
his apprentice for 5 days at 16s per day	4		
William Forrester for 8 days at £1 per day	8		
a barrel of tar	12		
100 treenails	1		
for carrying them to Port Seton		4	
7 days of a pitch pot at 2s per day		14	
nails, from William Leslie	7		
iron work, from Robert Hall	7	7	
Robert Ballentine, for bouts/bolts	6		
meat and drink to the carpenters and boys	40		
for carrying out may ballast	3	10	
for the report outward	2	18	
for dressing beer and water cask at Cockenzie	2	2	

	£	s	d
to the fishermen for carrying me aboard to sail		16	
2 barrels of beef	29		

	£	s	d
half a barrel of pork	11		
2cwt of biscuit at £6 per 100	12		
1½ hogsheads beer	9		
3 quarters of candles	2	5	
3 pecks of groats	2	8	
1 doz iron shot for the guns	2	8	
¼ hundred powder	16	16	
for bringing my men from Burntisland to Leith		14	
for going over again to sail, and for my mens' supper at Leith	1	16	
meat and drink to Murdie for keeping the ship at Burntisland	1	15	
2 hogsheads of water there		4	
2 pecks of peas		15	
a barrel of fresh fish at Holy Island	3	4	
2 oars for the boat	12		
100lb bread at Tynemouth	5	2	
12lb butter	2	8	
green bread	1	16	
1 bushel peas at Tynemouth	1	18	
2 tierces of beer there	7	16	
1 bushel peas at Harwich	1	16	
half a barrel of beer there	1	19	

Expenses at London

	£	s	d
paid to the two men-of-war's men that did help us to London from Harwich, after our own men being pressed	14	8	
for 5 men to liver our ship at London and to ballast her again	20	8	
ballast	12	18	
my report homeward, and light money	2	10	
clearing at the Customhouse	14	8	
to the man for getting out my cokets	4	16	
for my protection	20	4	
for putting my bill on the Exchange		18	
a hand lantern	1	4	
9lb candles	2		
to the pumpmaker for pump nails and pump boxes	4	2	

Page Twenty

	£	s	d
for dressing the compasses and glasses		18	

	£	s	d
a cann and a ladle		10	
1 doz spoons for the ship's use		18	
for dressing our beer and water cask		12	
for mending the kettle		6	
cartridge paper, small shot and match	1		
a new hawser and half a new cable	138	6	
bread and peas	36		
beer and wharfage	29	12	6
beef	45	18	
mending the sails	6	15	2
serviettes for the ship's use	1	19	
for my extraordinary expenses for procuring goods and passengers	18		
my mens wages;			
Adam Burnett	60		
John Dycks	13	10	
Thomas Turnbull	13	10	
Murdie Mackloud	13	10	
William Forrester, carpenter	15		
to myself	84		

Expenses at Gravesend

	£	s	d
to the Searchers	9	12	
to the gunner of the fort		6	
2 half barrels of beer	3	12	
6 great loaves for the passengers	1	4	
for mending the crans of the bowsprit	3	12	
6lb candles	1	4	
1 bushel peas	1	16	
40lb fresh beef	5		
a Gamlet [gimlet]		3	
1½ bushels turnips		12	
for my sailing orders	4	4	

Expenses at Yarmouth

	£	s	d
1 stone 3lb beef at 2s per stone	13	9	
a leg of mutton		18	
¾ hundred of biscuit at £5 8s per 100	4	1	
1 bushel peas	1	16	
a half hogshead and a tierce of beer	7		

Page Twenty-one

	£	s	d
2 stone of beef	2	8	
water		6	
a sprit for the boat		6	
a boats dish		2	
paid in exchange of a hogshead		8	
average of the whole voyage upwards conform 1/3	8	8	

Expenses at Leith

	£	s	d
for my report	2	18	
a boat to tow in the ship to the harbour	1	16	
for berthage at the quay to unload	2	18	
flag money	1	10	
to Robert Allan for anchorage and beaconage, shore			
dues and entry	11	16	8
plankage	1	4	
meat and drink to my men and boys in time of loading the			
ship from 14 April (inclusive) until the 28th [April]	16	17	
expenses in seeking my freight	6		
to the Captain of the man-of-war	13	4	

Page Twenty-two

An account of the freight received for the forsaid voyage from Port Seton to London and likewise the account of the freight from London to Leith in the forsaid months

56 tuns of coal at £7 4s per tun	403
10 casks tallow	6
6 barrels herring	22
downward freight for the Commissioner's goods	186
for passengers	120
for freight of other particular parcels	180
for the freight of Captain Sanderson, which he still owes me	36
for two passengers that owe me 10s	6

Freight £968 4s

Charges £947 13s 2d

Profit   £20 10s 10d

The George of Port Seton

An account of money disbursed for the use of my voyage from Methill with a lading of great coal; from the last of July to 9 December 1690

	£	s	d
Mrs Tait, for meat and drink to my men, boys and carpenters from 8 April to last of July 1690	29	13	
David Durie for carpenters work	23	16	
Alexander Sands for half a barrel of pitch and half a barrel tar	15		
the Shoremaster at Methill for anchorage, beaconage and the report	4	11	4
the Buckers for pilotage out and in to the Methill	3		
fresh fish and butter there	3	4	
casting my ballast over the quay	1	16	
whins for drying the ship		16	
4 men for carrying the ship from Leith to Methill	8	8	
anchorage at Burntisland	1	3	4
meat and drink to my men and boys there	20	18	
a pump breck and a quart of tar	1	4	
a leg of fresh beef at Burntisland	3	14	
2½ barrels of beef	37	10	
3 pecks groats	3	12	
200lb bread at £8 per 100	16		
2 teirces and half a hogshead of beer	11		
1 barrel of ale	2	8	
fresh beef for the passengers	1	4	
26 fish at 7s each	9	2	
12lb butter at 4s 6d per lb	2	19	
a firlot of peas	1	10	
a cooper for hooping the beer and water cask	1	2	
fresh fish at Holy Island		16	6
to the Captain of the man-of-war for my orders	4	9	
half a hogshead of beer at Yarmouth	3		
half a cwt of bread there	3		
anchorage at Harwich		6	
the gunner of the fort for my sign and for showing my coket		12	
4lb of butter there	1	9	
nails	9		

Expenses at London

	£	s	d
my report inward	3	7	
light money	6	1	

	£	s	d
20 last of ballast	12		
2 men to help liver our coal, being in haste	1	13	
114lb ropes at 27s 6d per 100	18	12	
8lb rosin for our masts and 6lb foul butter	1	11	
to put my bill on the Exchange		18	
my report outward	1	10	
beer and wharfage	30	16	

Page Twenty-four

	£	s	d
fresh beef	39		
an iron pump staff and some rudder nails	1	12	
to the block maker	3	6	
3 carpenters 2 days at 3s 6d ster per day	12	12	
Mr White for a barrel of tar and 4 bolts of reids	14	12	
the baker for bread and peas	26	2	
1 stone candles	3	4	
the sailmaker for mending the sails	[	]	
to the Customhouse when I cleared	14	8	
to the Broker that clears out	4	16	

To my mens wages

	£	s	d
Benjamin Robertson	48		
John Kerr	60		
John Fluckert	17		
David Shortis	33		
James Shade	30		
myself	72		
my extraordinary expenses	12		
to the Searchers at Gravesend	9	12	
to the gunner of the fort		6	
fresh beef for the passengers	7	4	
turnips, cabbage and carrots	1	16	
a sounding lead		15	
soft bread for the passengers		18	
one hundred and a quarter of beef at Yarmouth	10	4	
¾ of a hundred biscuit there	4	4	

	£	s	d
to the Customhouse at Scarborough for the entry of the wreck	18		

The George of Port Seton

	£	s	d
my mens diet at Scarborough	3		
to my men to carry them home	12	9	
to the gunner of Harwich fort for shewing my coket		12	
for saving the rigging and carrying it from the wreck			
to Scarborough	96		
to the entry of the wreck;			
paid at the Customhouse at Scarborough per receipt	18		

Page Twenty-five

An account of freight received for the forsaid freight to Londonfor the last of July 1690 to 9 December 1690

	£	s	d
for upward freight to London by bulk, received	564		
for the hold and rigging of the ship when she was lost,			
received	480		

Freight etc £1044

Expenses   £876 0s 8d

Profit   £167 19s 4d

Page Twenty-six

James Forrester – Debit

	£	s	d
due by me to the owners for the voyage from Port Seton to Greenock and Norway from the month of July 1687 to the month of March 1688	161	12	
to them for the voyage from Port Seton to London from the month of May to the month of July the the year 1688	45	10	6
to them for the voyage from 1 November 1689 to April 1690	20	10	10
to them for the voyage from Methill from last of July to 9 December 1690, when the ship was lost	167	19	4

Total £395 11s 8d

	£	s	d

James Forrester – Credit

due by the owners to me for my mens wages from Campveere
to Norway and from there to Port Seton upon the owners

	£	s	d
account; from March to the last of May 1687	235	8	
to Mr Alexander Droumand per account of the ship	60		
for a new hat for his man	7	4	
due by the owners to me in the voyage from Port Seton to London from July to the last of September 1688	42	18	4
due by them to me in the voyage from October to December 1688	145	2	
due by them to me in the voyage from Elphinstone to Rotterdam; from April to the last of June, 1689	214	10	
due by them to me in the voyage from Wemyss to Campveere from July to the last of September 1689	80	8	8
due by them to me for the Light of May for eight voyages at £3 15s per voyage	30		
for seven voyages, to John Adair	17	10	

Total £833 9s

Owing by owners to James Forrester – £437 17s 4d

Appendix 2

Extract from a page of the accounts

By courtesy of Edinburgh City Archives, ref. ECA/SL86/3/2.

The following illustration is a copy of a page in the accounts which shows the expenditure incurred on a voyage undertaken by the *George* from Port Seton to Rotterdam between October and December 1688. It was chosen because it illustrates the wide range of functions carried out by the master in the purchase of food, authorising repairs, paying men to load the ship and payment of harbour charges in Rotterdam. Forrester must have carried a considerable amount of money on his person at all times in order to make these payments, for it was unlikely that the ship carried a safe.

This is a record made by an educated man who was capable of keeping a neat and accurate set of accounts – a skill which was not common in the latter part of the seventeenth century.

Ane Accompt of moneÿ disbursed for ẏᵉ use of my Jagga
from new Port Seton to Rotterdam with ane loading of small
Coals upon ẏᵉ account of James Smith in Tranent and James Watt
in Prestoun Pans from ẏᵉ moneth of october to ẏᵉ first of november
in ẏᵉ 1608   lib | s | 8

		£	s	d
Impᵗ for Caiving out my balast		3	6	
Itᵐ for ane barrell of Tarr		8	4	
Itᵐ for nails		3	6	
Itᵐ for 2 Carpinters 4½ daÿ		37	10	
Itᵐ for 3 barrells of beef and for Caiving it to Port Seton		10	16	
Itᵐ for beer			14	
Itᵐ for triming our heid and matter Cables		9		
Itᵐ for a Shind		10	16	
Itᵐ for two hundred weight of breid		2	16	
Itᵐ for 4 pecks of Groats		2	10	
Itᵐ for halfe a boll of piese		5	2	4
Itᵐ for clackbridge		5	4	
Itᵐ for a still to ẏᵉ gloutters and to ẏᵉ beamer		5	10	
Itᵐ for ẏᵉ fisher men for helping ẏᵉ Shipp out		12	15	
Itᵐ to James Grotter for meat and drink to ẏᵉ Carpenter and boys		5		
Itᵐ for my Coket		3	4	
Itᵐ for ane stone of Candells			8	
Itᵐ for ane pound of thairns		2	6	
Itᵐ for ane pass from ẏᵉ Cuncell		2 8	12	
Itᵐ for my pylitage ober ẏᵉ mase and from ẏᵉ briggs to Rotterdam		1 4		
Itᵐ paÿt pylits for getting my Cabell and Anchor againe at ẏᵉ pitt		5	5	
Itᵐ for twa dusen of Cabluk			4	
Itᵐ for ane beer barn			7	
Itᵐ for ane pound of butter		4	12	
Itᵐ for half a barroll of herring		4	8	
Itᵐ for mending our harth		28	6	
Itᵐ for a new Gibb		8	6	
Itᵐ for 64 pound of Ropes		1	6	
Itᵐ for clackbridge in Holland		15	15	
Itᵐ for 20 last of balast		15	9	
Itᵐ for beer		10	1	
Itᵐ for breid			10	
Itᵐ for ane bottle of traine oyls for ẏᵉ Lamps		5	5	4
Itᵐ for 4 pound of Candells		5	3	
Itᵐ for damadge		5	15	
Itᵐ for pylitay ober ẏᵉ mase homward			16	
Itᵐ for helping ẏᵉ Ship in to ẏᵉ herber		258 15	5	

Appendix 3

Inventory of the George

This document was submitted as evidence in a case held in the Admiralty Court in 1703. Reproduced by kind permission of the Keeper of the Records of Scotland.

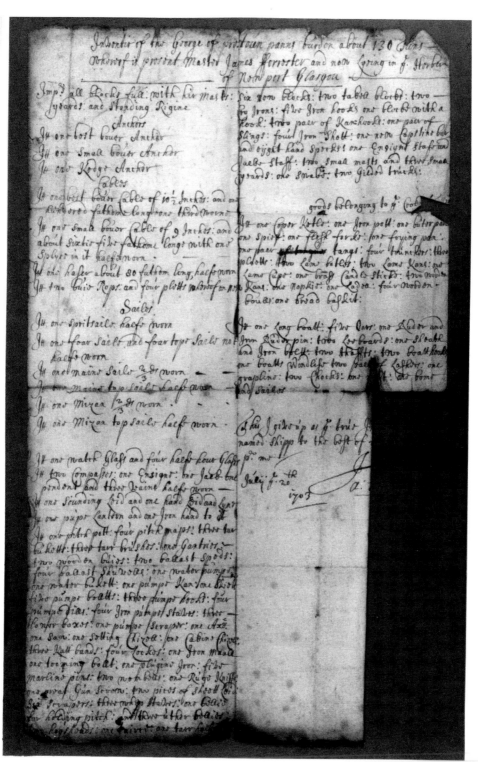

Capture of an Orkney sloop by a privateer in 1709

Source: PRO Vol CXIII No. 43 (Reproduced by permission of the Public Record Office on behalf of the Controller of Her Majesty's Stationary Office)

Edinburgh 5th April 1709

To the Honourable William Lowndes Esq at the Treasury Chambers, Whitehall.

Upon the 22nd March last, wee have you an account of the unfortunate news wee received, from our officers of the Orkney Sloop being taken, by the French, in Cromarty Bay; since which Mr Tomlinson Mate of that Sloop, with some of Her sailors, put a shoar at that place, are come to us, on foot, from thence in a very sad condition, and given us an account of the manner of Her being taken, which wee have caused to be turned into an affadavit, & transmitted to you, for your further information.

Mr Crookshanks the Comptroller Generall will deliver you this, as also a presentment for Mr John Muirhead, which we pray you will lay before the Lord High Treasurer.

(Signed by the Commissioners for Customs)

James Tomlinson Chief Mate, Willoughby Hall Carpenter, and John Forshaw Steward, lately belonging to the Orkney Sloop make Oath, that on Thursday the twenty seventh day of January last they set sail from Shields or Tinmouth Haven ... on Thursday morning wee found ourselves in Murray Firth where wee saw several fishing boats, on which we made a warfe with the antient and fired a gun for a pilot, and one John Wood came on board brought us up to Cromerty and there wee got a new missen mast and refitted, and on the last day of February wee set sail from Cromerty in order to come for Leith, and sailed up almost the length of Aberdeen but the wind took us short, and forced the same vessell back again into Cromerty, where we lay wind bound until the thirteenth of March, and aobut nyne or tenn of the clock at night a Briganteen came into Cromerty and wee hailed him with a speaking Trumpet from whence he was, and he answered us again with his voice (wind and tide bringing him on at a great rate) that his name was Ralph Waugh from Newcastle, and the Captain being very well acquainted with him as he haveing been a surveyor of the said shipp upon her being launcht, and the said Waugh a little before having taken in a loading of beer and fish at Findhorne about twelve miles off for Lisbon, we were certain it was the same shipp the same Waugh sailed from Newcastle, whereupon the Captain ordered the boat to be lowered out of the tackles and six of the best hands to be ready in her in order to go aboard the said vessell and inquire what news at sea, and if there were many privateers upon the coast, or what was his reason for comeing in there, he haveing given out he was bound for Lisbon, and this deponent Willoughby Hall say'th that he was in the boat and went along with her to the Briganteen, and the Captain ordered this deponent to goe aboard, whereupon he step't into the Briganteen, and this deponent was no sooner aboard but two men seiz'd him, and imediately this deponent asked for Mr Waugh and they told this deponent he was a comeing, and imediately this deponent broke from the two men, and went aft the shipp and there saw lying on the deck twelve or fourteen Frenchmen with small armes, whereupon this deponent runn to the side of the shipp and call'd to the Captain and men in the boat to put off for that they were betray'd by Waugh, and imediatley as the Captain was puting off the boat, there came about twenty men all with small arms and presented at the Captain and the crew, the boat being within two or three feet of the end of their musketts, and said if they wold not come aboard instantly they would shoot them, whereupon they were forced aboard, and this deponent went forward to call to the rest of the crew aboard the Sloop, but a person follow'd this deponent and claped a pistol to his breast and said he would shoot him dead if he cry'd out to them, and afterwards they putt about fifteen or sixteen Frenchmen into the boat and went to the Sloop, and this deponent James Tomlinson further deposeth that he was standing on the quarter deck with the boason when he saw the boat coming to the Sloop again hee hail'd her and they answered ho-ho which is a terme us'd by sailors, which made him believe it was their own boats crew comeing aboard again, and this deponent had order'd some of the men to stand aft with a rope to heave into the boat, and this deponent and the boason stood at the ladder foor to receive the Captain, and the first thing this deponent saw was two pistolls snapt at him but neither of them went off, and the boason went forward into the forecastle, and a pistoll went off after him but misd him, and imediately they forced this deponent and the rest of the crew into the hold, but the cabbin boy being in the Captain's cabbin makeing a fire hearing the noise upon deck and a pistoll going off took up a blunderbuss loaded with about twelve pistoll balls fired the same but did no execution being all in darkness except a light in the Captain's cabin.

Index

Index